GREAT SUFFOLK STORIES

CAROL TWINCH

THE AUTHOR

BORN IN SUFFOLK, the author travelled widely before returning to farm in her native county with her husband and two children. She has contributed to numerous magazines and newspapers, worked in local radio and on television and is the author of books on agricultural and social history as well as handbooks on poultry and sheep management. Carol Twinch has also published a number of short stories and she currently works as an editor and book reviewer on *Images,* the Ipswich Arts Association magazine. She lives near Saxmundham.

GREAT SUFFOLK STORIES

CAROL TWINCH

Fort Publishing Ltd

First published in 2003 by Fort Publishing Ltd, 12 Robsland Avenue,
Ayr, KA7 2RW

Printed by Bell and Bain, Glasgow

Typeset by S. Fairgrieve (0131-658-1763)

ISBN 0-9544461-2-7

CONTENTS

PREFACE   ix

ONE   'GOT ANY GUM, CHUM?'   1

TWO   'YOU CAN TAKE THE GIRL OUT OF
           IPSWICH': SUFFOLK'S GI BRIDES   14

THREE   CLOSE ENCOUNTERS: THE ALIEN
           INVASION OF SUFFOLK   23

FOUR   HAUNTED SUFFOLK   34

FIVE   SUFFOLK DAUGHTERS   45

SIX   SUFFOLK SONS   56

SEVEN   CLUBBED TO DEATH: THE MURDER
           OF SUFFOLK'S RICHEST WOMAN   75

EIGHT   WHO KILLED ROSE HARSENT?   86

NINE   MURDER AT THE RED BARN   99

TEN   THE WAR AGAINST TITHE   107

ELEVEN   A NIGHT TO REMEMBER:
           JULIA CAVENDISH AND THE *TITANIC*   121

TWELVE   DEATH IN THE SKIES   128

THIRTEEN   GENIUS: BENJAMIN BRITTEN AND
           THE STORY OF SNAPE   135

FOURTEEN	SIR ALF	145
FIFTEEN	ON THE COAST	158
SIXTEEN	FOR THE LOVE OF WILL	167
SEVENTEEN	CHURCHYARD TALES	181
EIGHTEEN	BOUDICCA: THE WARRIOR QUEEN	196
BIBLIOGRAPHY		*207*

PREFACE

IT IS SAID that writing about what you know is a double-edged sword and that collections such as *Great Suffolk Stories* should be written not by a native but by an outsider, who might be thought to bring balance and objectivity to the subject. If that is the case, I am unsuited since my family has lived and farmed in Suffolk for at least three hundred years. It is folklore that unless your family has roots in Suffolk for something approaching that length of time, you are a 'newcomer'. Suffolkers do not think of this as unwelcoming, merely a precautionary measure of an ancient people who have never given their trust easily. Such things, though, can be overcome. In conversation with a stranger tending graves in a Suffolk church-yard we got talking about this peculiar Suffolk defence mechanism and he laughed. He had retired there, he said, but had never had any trouble being accepted. By chance there were lots of old family graves there with the same name as his and local people had always assumed he was 'one of them'. Of course he had no connections at all but while he never said so, he also never denied it!

Suffolk is the southern part of East Anglia and, logically enough, the place where the 'south folk' live. It is characterised by ancient market towns, rolling farmland, villages that still have thatched and colour-washed cottages, and both town and country boast landmark churches, ancient and modern. The south of the county is only seventy miles from London and it measures about sixty miles west to east, from the horse-racing town of Newmarket to the North Sea, and forty miles south to north from John

Constable's Stour Valley to the fringes of Broadland. Its area is about 1,500 square miles, almost a million acres. The largest town is Ipswich, whose name is derived from the Anglo-Saxon 'Gipes Wic' (more commonly 'Gypeswick' and meaning a town at the mouth of a river). It is bounded on the south by the landmark of the Orwell Bridge which was, at the time of its opening in 1982, one of the largest concrete structures in Europe.

Until 1974 Suffolk was divided into two – East Suffolk, Ipswich its largest town, and West Suffolk where Bury St Edmunds was the principal town, the site of what was in pre-Reformation times, the most influential monastery in Suffolk. Although it is administered now as one county there is still an invisible east–west divide and not a little rivalry.

Family names, such as Garrett, Cobbold and Mobbs, turn up in more than one story, while mention of Suffolk's internationally renowned poet George Crabbe runs through the book like a silver thread and disposes of the theory that men are rarely prophets in their own country. Crabbe is not considered a great poet ('look in vain for layered metaphors' wrote one critic) but he was at least an original one. Unsurprisingly, since he was born in Aldeburgh and came from a long line of Crabbes who lived and worked along the shores of Suffolk, his greatest influence was the sea. Once, not having seen the sea for a considerable time, he embarked on a sixty-mile journey purely for the pleasure of looking at it.

Another strand that weaves its way through the chapters is the sea itself. Stand on the crumbling cliffs at North Cove on a raw and windy day and feel the salty might of the sea as it batters your face and clothes. Put a shoulder into the driving rain, each drop like a sharp needle stinging and tormenting your skin, and look down at the fallen earth and watch as the overhanging grass tumbles down to the shore below. Draw your collar up against the cold, clammy sea-rain trickling down your neck and remember Crabbe's words 'The ocean roar whose greedy waters devour the lessening shore'. Coastal erosion is a fact of life along the Suffolk coast.

The people I have written about are a mixed lot: some were born here and made good elsewhere, and others adopted Suffolk as their home. Peggy Cole, for instance, is a Suffolk 'gal' through and through, while others like Doreen Wallace and Frankie Dettori came here by fortune or from choice. Wallis Simpson wrote Felixstowe into history purely by chance, whilst Sir John Mills has strong associations with the county not least by having had an Ipswich theatre named after him. The Sir John Mills Theatre and its company Eastern Angles are currently celebrating twenty years of taking theatre to the towns and villages of East Anglia (and often beyond). Founded by Ivan Cutting, the Angles' artistic director, its first production was *When the Boats Come In* – about the history of the Lowestoft herring industry – since when Black Shuck, Margaret Catchpole, the Tithe War and Boudicca have featured among the company's productions.

The special relationship that has existed between America and Suffolk for hundreds of years deserves more space than is found here, and there has been no room for the historic figures that made history across the Atlantic. In 1602 Bartholomew Gosnold from Otley led an exploratory expedition to what was then called 'the north parts of Virginia'. He went on to Cape Cod and named Martha's Vineyard in memory of his daughter who had recently died. A few years later, in 1610, the borough of Ipswich bought shares in the Virginia Company, which financed voyages to America.

In 1634 a Hadleigh preacher named Nathaniel Ward emigrated to Ipswich, Massachusetts. Prior to the English arriving there in 1633 a small tribe of Agawam Indians lived on the site but the settlement name was changed from Agawam to Ipswich because 'English settlements preferred English names to Indian names in order to be considered "proper".' Nathaniel Ward was asked to draft a code of laws for use in the new colony. In 1641 his document of 100 laws was completed and was the first such set ever to be used in the United States of America. Nathaniel Ward was also the first American novelist and wrote *A Simple Cobler of Aggawam*, published in England in 1646. It was very successful, probably because he poked fun at the simple life of the colonists.

Since the early settlement days other links had been forged or maintained, though the two cultures grew and developed so differently that when, during the Second World War, three million Americans passed through Suffolk it was as if they came from different planets. The story of the United States Army Air Force in no way detracts from the heroics of the British services but is intended to highlight the extraordinary effects of having nineteen new air bases, and a quarter of a million Americans, appearing in Suffolk in just six months. These wartime airfields are, by and large, returned to agriculture – that at Horham bought and reclaimed by my father in the early 1960s (although one of the old runways is still used for light aircraft). One of the best places to go for an understanding of the intense and complicated relationship between Suffolk and the Americans is the Rose Garden in the Abbey grounds at Bury St Edmunds.

There can be few professional football teams that have as loyal a following as Ipswich Town. The players, managers and board officials are accorded unconditional loyalty and support, and it goes without saying that head and shoulders above most other Suffolk heroes stand Alf Ramsey and Bobby Robson. Writing about Sir Alf and the 1966 World Cup brought back memories, not least that my cousin's wedding took place on the day of the final. As we are a family of avid and enthusiastic football followers, the day was not without problems, especially as one of my uncles had taught Geoff Hurst at school. At the time, substituting the raw and relatively unproven Hurst for the legendary Jimmy Greaves caused a storm of press criticism. It evaporated when Hurst scored a hat trick and England's all-important fourth goal and gave rise to the immortal words, 'They think it's all over . . . it is now.' With one exception the English bench exploded, but Alf Ramsey remained in his seat, his eyes fixed on the pitch. He told the man in front of him, 'Sit down, I can't see.' Alf was never a man who danced on the touchline.

Inevitably the decline of agriculture will continue to affect the county so that places like Easton Farm Park and Baylham Rare Breeds Farm, and events like 'Power of the Past' at Wantisden, are needed to keep alive the character that has sustained Suffolk since the days of Boudicca. The ability to merge tradition with modernity is best demonstrated at the annual Suffolk Show, which has been at the heart of county life since 1831, and at the Museum of East Anglian Life at Stowmarket which succeeds in blending the old and new through activities and exhibitions. The problem of absorbing changing times and an increasing population without losing local identity, and planning growth without damaging ancient culture and heritage, remains a huge challenge.

I would like to acknowledge the assistance of the following people and organisations: Lorna Andersen (USA), Michael Brander, Norman Burtenshaw OBE, William Cavendish, Peggy Cole MBE, Eastern Angles Theatre Company, Ipswich Town Football Club, A. A. (Tony) and Thelma Mobbs, Jean Moss (Ipswich, Massachusetts, USA), Ipswich Museum Services, David Kindred, Long Shop Museum, Moyse's Hall Museum, Norfolk and Suffolk Aviation Museum, 390th Bomber Group Memorial Air Museum, RMS *Queen Mary* Museum (USA), Vincent O'Neil (USA), Newmarket Racecourses, Sir Bobby Robson CBE, Robert and Pearl Simper, Suffolk County Council Library Services, Suffolk Horse Society.

Carol Twinch
Rendham, 2003

ONE

'Got any gum, chum?'

BETWEEN 1942 AND 1945 about three million American military and auxiliary men and women passed through Britain. Because of the proximity of Suffolk airfields to mainland Europe, the numbers multiplied so that by the end of April 1944 there were 71,000 Americans in the county. Since there were, according to the 1931 census, 401,000 inhabitants in Suffolk, give or take a slight increase in the population, one in seven people living in Suffolk for most of the Second World War was an American.

The village of Coney Weston, the nearest to USAAF Knettishall, had a population of around 300 in 1942: the following year an airfield was built and the 300 swelled to almost 3,000 American servicemen and auxiliary personnel. At Parham (USAAF Framlingham) the population went from 325 to 3,325 – more than ten Americans to one local.

In July 1942 the first American B-17 bombers and P-38 fighters and crews arrived and by the middle of 1944 the 8th Air Force had grown to become the biggest military air fleet ever seen. By the end of the war there were around 1,300 aircraft flying from over thirty airfields in Suffolk.

It was the Japanese naval attack on US Navy and Army bases at Pearl Harbor in 1941 that brought America into the war. Plans were made for the US forces to be moved to Britain and the United States Army Air Force (USAAF) wanted bases which would place their long-range bombers as close to Germany as possible. A saturation air campaign was planned. The USAAF would bomb by day from bases in the east of Suffolk and the RAF would bomb by night, taking off from stations in the west. The RAF departed for Germany at sunset and as they returned the Americans would take off and assemble into large formations before heading east. Due to advanced technology the USA's Flying Fortresses, the first all-metal bombers, could fly at higher altitudes and operate more accurate bombsights than their British counterparts, while the Liberators could go faster and carry more bombs. The large numbers involved meant planes taking off at twenty-second intervals. This was an exceedingly dangerous part of the mission and there were occasions when the wingtips were less than twenty feet apart.

To the war-weary and hungry population of Suffolk, the men of the 8th Air Force were exotic, well-fed, smartly uniformed and sounded as though they had just stepped out of a movie. The average age of the American crews was twenty-two. This exotic, gum-chewing slice of youth from the New World flew in to startle and scandalise the rural communities of the Old World, much of it very old indeed. The arrival of Hollywood in a rural Suffolk still run largely along Edwardian lines both shocked and amazed the natives – and the 'Yanks' thought they had been sent to the dark side of the moon. 'Merrie England' was still a land where cars were a rarity, farming practices were much as they had been for hundreds of years and few farmhouses had electricity. Many rural communities still drew their water from wells and outside 'privies' were the accepted norm.

In addition to the existing airbases there were nineteen new USAAF airbases constructed in Suffolk during 1942 and 1943 for the use of the 8th Army Air Force. In the west of the county were Knettishall, Honington, Great Ashfield, Bury St Edmunds, Rattlesden, Wattisham, Lavenham, Sudbury and Raydon. In the east were Bungay (or Flixton), Metfield, Halesworth (or Holton), Horham, Eye, Mendlesham, Framlingham (or Parham), Leiston, Debach and Martlesham Heath. Elveden Hall was Divisional Headquarters for the 8th Air Force. In 1943 Woodbridge airfield was used as an Emergency Landing Ground and the 356th Fighter wing arrived at Martlesham.

It is an easy enough matter to name names, and play with numbers, but in 1942 these nineteen military establishments did not actually exist and their construction comprised entirely new developments on virgin sites. At existing RAF stations, such as at Stradishall (which was upgraded from an airfield begun in 1935), Mildenhall, Honingham and Wattisham, the grass runways had to be reinforced with concrete in order to absorb the take-off and landing pressure of huge bomber aircraft. The main runways needed to be over a mile long, and in addition subsidiary runways, hardstanding for huts, control towers and other airfield necessities, as well as accommodation for the construction crews and administrators, and base hospitals had to be constructed.

East Anglia's proximity to continental Europe, its flat and open geography, and absence of large urban centres, made it the obvious choice for the launch of the bomber offensive against Germany. Considering the almost inconceivable intrusion these new military establishments were going to cause, Suffolkers might have been forgiven for thinking that it was they, not Germany, who were in the sights of an offensive.

Villages in the immediate vicinity came under intolerable strain from the unfamiliar activity, and particularly the noise, as heavy construction traffic negotiated winding, narrow country lanes and earth-moving equipment began work. After the runways were built, homes were abandoned when it became impossible to live under the incessant drone of the B-17 and B-24 engines. At certain times of the day the skies above Suffolk were filled with anything up to a hundred aircraft. During the height of operations around a thousand planes would form a line up to a hundred miles long, their vapour trails covering the sky and obliterating the sun. Those living in the houses and cottages that had been left alongside the runways were in mortal danger every day of their lives. Crash landings were common as most American pilots had learned to fly in wide-open spaces, such as Texas or Arizona, where clouds and poor visibility were unheard of. One young airman commented that the English airfields were 'the size of a dime!' The greatest peril was the crash landing of returning damaged bombers, particularly in bad weather. Overshooting the runways in fog was a particular hazard. In 1943 a Liberator exploded after take-off at Bungay and crashed into the nearby village of Mendham, killing all the crew.

At Horham several houses in the surrounding parishes were abandoned including Thorpe Hall, an Elizabethan hunting lodge once used by Henry VIII. Horham was one of those airfields that had begun life, in 1941, as an RAF base but was reallocated to the Americans in 1942.

Debris was scattered over a wide area following the horrific mid-air inferno that killed Lieutenant Joseph Kennedy, son of the former US ambassador to Britain and elder brother of the future American President, John F. Kennedy. On the afternoon of 12 August 1944 Kennedy's Liberator took off from the Fersfield-Winfarthing airfield on a top-secret mission. Just as it flew over Blythburgh, before heading out to sea, the aircraft exploded in a fireball suspended momentarily in mid-air before shattering and disintegrating into millions of burning fragments which landed over a wide area.

In Dick Wickham's *The War at my Door*, eye-witness David Bacon recalls watching two Liberators taking off from Holton: 'Taking off one morning and forming up into their formations . . . two Liberators touched wings, both crashed in Henham woods one each side of the Beccles to Blythburgh road. One crashed into the tops of some pine trees levelling them all off. The other one crashed into a pit and caught fire.' The Halesworth fire brigade attended but as they fought the blaze the bomb load on one of the aircraft blew up, killing all seventeen firemen as well as the aircrew from both planes. 'I went to the crash site', said David, 'to have a look. It was terrible. There were parachutes and bits and pieces all hanging up in the trees. Terrible.'

At Metfield the base's bomb dump blew up killing at least five men and severely damaging several aircraft and surrounding huts. The explosion was heard for miles around and the Group stood down while an inquiry was held to investigate the cause. Sabotage was suspected but after four days it was decided that the explosion had been an accident.

In 1944 the crew of a B-17 miraculously escaped as their plane blew up after crash landing just short of Wattisham runway, still carrying twenty 250 lb unexploded bombs. Returning from a raid over France, the B-17 was caught in the flak, sustaining lethal damage and jamming the bomb doors. Soon after impact, in a field next to the officers' married quarters at Great Bricett, the whole lot went up seconds after the pilot had been dragged free.

Near Framlingham, home to the 390th Bombardment Group, a Flying Fortress crashed onto the Methodist Chapel at Parham on 27 December 1944. Michael Hurlock, who lived at nearby Bridge Farm, remembers the window shattering and the glass going all over the food on the kitchen table. Parishioners reported finding 'limbs of bodies for days afterwards'.

It has been said, with little exaggeration, that the coming of the Americans to Suffolk heralded the end of a centuries-old age of innocence. Long-held beliefs and customs had certainly been challenged during the inter-war years, but in Suffolk the old ways died hard. This shattering of 'ye olde Suffolke' was quite literal. Where a site had been chosen by the men in Whitehall the first thing that happened was a flotilla of bowler-hatted men with clipboards arriving to survey the area. But 'the area' was not a piece of convenient waste ground – it was generally someone's farm. Understandably, farmers were reluctant to give up land just as it was becoming profitable for the first time since 1918, as the challenge to feed the home population, deprived of previous plentiful imports, had to be met. The Air Ministry, therefore, needed to requisition farmland before construction work could begin. A bomber base took up a lot of space and many thousands of acres were required.

Construction work began soon after requisition papers, either to compulsorily buy or rent the land, were served by the War

Department. Immediately the peace and quiet of the countryside was well and truly shattered. Most of the bases took six months to build, contractors bringing hardcore from wherever they could get it. Rubble from the bombed streets of London and Birmingham arrived in Suffolk by day and night on trains and lorries and was supplemented by shingle from nearby beaches. Trees were cut down, their roots blown up, and reservoirs built. These were needed for the water required not only for the construction process but also to service the finished base where numbers up to and exceeding 3,000 personnel would live.

By the time the American troops arrived the Suffolk landscape had altered out of all recognition. The county was a mosaic of military establishments that had grown like mushrooms and displaced the real mushrooms, the cattle and the sheep in the meadows and fields, which were obliterated from sight. These 'islands' of American technology contrasted peculiarly with the surrounding countryside, which still had its 'ye olde worlde' look of thatched cottages and impenetrable hedges, outdoor lavatories and paraffin, or 'Tilley', lamps to see by. In the countryside it was rare for houses to have running (piped) water and rainwater was collected for the weekly bath. People found it strange to travel along a familiar road and then, in the matter of a few yards, to be transported across the Atlantic.

The two sectors of Suffolk society that gave the Americans the biggest welcome were the children and the young women. The local children congregated at vantage points where they were likely to see the newly arrived strangers and listen, enthralled, to the accent so unfamiliar in Suffolk but familiar to anyone who went to the cinema. Those who had never seen an American movie were just as fascinated and eager to catch up. Before long they began to mimic the servicemen, using their slang and asking each other 'Got any gum, chum?' Small groups of boys would spend hours hanging around the base perimeters, watching the goings on, entranced by the sheer excitement of it all. Many took up plane spotting and made endless sketches of their favourite Liberators or Flying Fortresses, together with each aircraft's nickname that was painted across the outside of the cockpit. The boys made lists of the nicknames such as 'No Guts – No Glory', '£5 with breakfast' (reputedly the going rate for a high-class London prostitute), 'My Aching Back' (showing a scantily clad female), 'Kentucky Belle', 'Hurry Home Honey' and 'In the Mood'. They liked the names given to the various units: 'The Bungay Buckeroos', 'Helton's Hell Cats' (named after Debach's first commanding officer, Colonel Elbert Helton), 'The Yoxford Boys' and Halesworth's 'Zemke's Wolfpack' (named after the 56th Flight Group's leader, Colonel Hubert Zemke).

When the Americans began to mix off-base, the children fell under their spell and loved their easy informality. The Yanks were friendly towards the children, and would speak to anyone they met, unlike the rather more formal English, while the sweets and comics that they handed out made them friends for life. Their attempts to ape the English accent kept the children in fits of laughter as they tried to say 'Good show!' and 'Actually, old chap!' and talked about being 'browned off'. Many were equally bemused by the Suffolk accent, which was different to anything they heard on the BBC, and teased the aeroplane-mad youths about the way they spoke.

Anxious that schoolchildren should be introduced to America and its customs by an official route, in 1943 the Board of Education commissioned 100,000 copies of *Meet the U.S. Army* for circulation in schools. American servicemen who had been teachers in civilian life were asked to visit schools and give informal talks about their home and way of life.

For some those years of meeting the Americans, and watching the 'Forts' and Liberators take off and land, left an indelible and abiding impression. One who stood and watched from the perimeter fence was Roger Freeman who as a boy in 1943 witnessed the arrival of the USAAF in East Anglia. He is now a leading authority on US warplanes, the airmen who flew them, and the Second World War operations in which they were involved and one of the most respected historians of the 8th Air Force.

For the young women the coming of the Americans was a dream come true. Although the new bases were self-sufficient in just about everything they needed in the way of supplies, they had to find their entertainment off-base. Although later in the war the larger bases equipped themselves with clubs and movie theatres, the local 'flicks' or 'flea pit' in the nearby town was still likely to have a greater attraction since there would be the possibility of female company.

Here the lowly bicycle came into its own and prices of second-hand bicycles soared. Because of the sheer size of the bases and the complete absence of public transport, bicycles became the chief mode of transport not just for the locals but for many GIs, some of whom had never ridden one before. They were also used to driving on the right hand side of the road and this caused numerous accidents, especially on the way back to base from the local pub in the blackout. Whenever there was a dance or similar event planned the off-duty Americans would appear on their bicycles, to the dismay of the resident Lotharios. Where bicycles were in short supply the Americans often arrived 'three to a bike' gaining them a reputation for fun which contrasted them with the British officers, nicknamed 'Mr Frigidaire'.

The obvious attractions of the American servicemen to the local women were hardly likely to go unnoticed by the local males, and mothers and grandmothers shook their heads in despair. They chastised their daughters and granddaughters for having their heads 'turned' while the young men were naturally jealous and thoroughly put out. The girls shook their heads and laughed. They liked the 'Hi, beautiful!' and 'Hiya Baby!' greetings, and responded accordingly to the generous gifts of wartime luxuries, like chocolate, cigarettes and nylons, especially welcome as British women had already gone without these extras for three years. Even a lowly US private received £3 15s per week, while an ordinary RAF man earned only 17s. 6d per week. That made the American big spenders since they had four times as much to spend.

The young women, like the children, were amazed at the informality and sense of fun that the Americans exuded, and scandalised their elders by fraternising with them whenever they could. To the distress of Suffolk mothers everywhere their daughters began to exclaim 'Jeeze!' and 'Holy Cow!' and laugh hysterically when they heard the expression 'bum' for a no-good layabout. The nickname 'Yank' was soon incorporated into wartime jokes: 'What is it they say about American servicemen and British women's knickers?' 'One Yank and they're off!' During the war years the expression 'overpaid, over-sexed and over here!' was coined and is still used as an evocative reminder of how many parents saw the American invasion!

The second most popular form of entertainment in wartime Britain, after the 'pictures', was the Saturday night dance, already the highlight of weekly entertainment in towns and villages alike. Particularly popular for those outside the main towns were the dances held in the various Women's Land Army (WLA) or Women's Timber Corps (WTC) hostels, or those where Land Girls were invited in return onto the bases. These were the women recruited to replace men on the farms and in the forests, who performed extraordinary service in maintaining home supplies in the face of the sea blockade. There could be anything from ten to a hundred girls billeted in any one hostel so there was usually no shortage of partners for the new 'jitterbug' dancing – or jiving as it became known in England – which the Americans introduced, along with the slower, 'smooth' music which became known as 'the big band sound'. Dance, especially in rural areas, was central to the social life of the county and when notices began appearing in village halls proclaiming 'No Jitterbugging' they were largely ignored.

The legendary Glenn Miller and his Army Air Force Band toured all over England giving over 800 performances of which 500 were broadcast. He gave many live concerts in Suffolk including one at Horham to celebrate the two-hundredth bombing mission of the 95th Bomb Group. In August 1944, only four months before he was killed, Glenn Miller and his band went to Framlingham where they gave an evening concert on Parham airfield attended by over 6,000. They arrived in six B-17s and in addition to the base personnel there were nurses from a nearby military hospital, Land Army girls, civilians and women from the WACS, WRENS and WAFFS. The indelible memory of hearing 'Moonlight Serenade' and other evocative Miller tunes lives on in those who were there that night and at other concerts across the county.

Other well-known Americans, genuine movie stars, came over to entertain the troops, including Bob Hope, Vivien Leigh and Marlene Dietrich. Clarke Gable was a captain attached to the 351st Bomb Group, and he always joked that his greatest fear was that he would be shot down and Hitler would exhibit him in a cage. James Stewart was commanding officer of a Liberator Squadron, and one of his sergeants was Walter Matthau. Micky Rooney was one of many who enlisted to serve with a special unit of artists sent over to entertain the troops in Europe.

There were, naturally enough, differences between the servicemen of the 'friendly invasion' and both the local men and British servicemen which sometimes turned violent, usually when an off-duty American got into a fight in a pub. But there was, after all, a war on, and it was this that ultimately cemented relations between Suffolk and the USAAF. Aircrew could be stationed at the same base for anything from six months to a year and ground crew, who outnumbered the airmen twenty to one, often stayed for over a year.

In 1942 the American crews flew twenty-five missions before returning home but as the number of casualties increased and the war continued it was gradually increased to thirty-five. The men got to know local people and were known in the towns and villages by name and reputation. If they made a long series of successful flying missions they became local heroes. Friendships were forged, and when aircrew did not return from a bombing mission both communities mourned them. It was especially poignant when a serviceman had made friends with a local family, which often happened, and they would sadly be missing at Sunday lunch or in the local pub where many of them drank. Not all the men were single, many were happily married and missed their families. They, in particular, enjoyed joining the local choir, where many servicemen sang, and in some places dancing classes were held, such as those at Leiston. Anglo-American sports days were held in Saxmundham and at the Portman Road football ground in Ipswich.

After VE Day in 1945 the USAAF left Suffolk as quickly as it had arrived. With a few exceptions the airfields fell silent, the skies no longer hummed with the sound of the bombers and the towns and villages were suddenly without the twang of an American accent. Farewell parties were hurriedly convened and tears shed as goodbyes echoed across the deserted runways and the power was switched off in the control towers. Honington was the last to close, in 1946. On a wet, cold parade ground the Stars and Stripes were lowered for the last time and the keys handed back to the RAF. It is now an RAF regiment base and some of the old hangars remain.

It had not been all 'beer and skittles' by any means. There had been problems caused not only by the differences of culture but especially by their attitudes to the local women. In their pursuit of 'a cute piece of ass' GIs began to take advantage of the situation. It was not unusual for 'Snowdrops', the name given to the US military police on account of their white helmets, to be summoned to deal with airmen laying siege to a Land Army hostel. People were hurt and, inevitably, women were left to carry the consequences of affairs with servicemen who returned to America at the end of the war. In response to a profound and obvious need, the Transatlantic Children's Enterprise (TRACE) was founded by a former war bride in 1986 and, together with another group, War Babes, has been able to unite many of these war babies with their American fathers.

At the Imperial War Museum at Duxford the American Air Museum stands as a tribute to the American airmen who flew from Britain between 1942 and 1945 and to the 30,000 who gave their lives. Across Suffolk, in churches and beside the old airfields, are memorials to the servicemen of the 'Mighty Eighth', and at Bury St Edmunds the Old English Rose Garden was created through the generosity of Technical Sergeant John Appleby of Arkansas, USA. Based at Lavenham and Thorpe Abbots he spent his leisure time exploring Suffolk by bicycle, recording his experiences which he later published in *Suffolk Summer*, the royalties for which go to maintaining the garden in the Abbey Gardens close to the Cathedral.

A plaque that hangs in the borough offices commemorates another American, General F. W. Castle, who led the 3rd Airborne

Division during the Battle of the Bulge, Christmas Eve 1944, a mission from which he did not return.

Some of the nineteen airfields built during the 1940s now have museums and host Anglo-American reunions, which return year after year to Suffolk. In the summer of 2002 numerous events took place across the county including a reunion of seven veterans from the 34th Bomb Group. A Mustang fighter performed a number of fly-pasts as the men laid a wreath at the war memorial, near the A140, before revisiting Mendlesham in six American Jeeps to take a look at the Book of Remembrance in St Mary's Church. Pilot Herb Roy told the *East Anglian Daily Times:*

> I have reunions with some of the airmen in America but it is always special to come back to England where it all happened. It's hard to imagine when you see all the beautifully-restored old planes in museums that they used to come back covered in holes from flak fire and machine guns. There often wasn't any time to repair the damage so we would fly with the wind whistling through the cabin and the temperature down to minus 15C. Missions could be up to 12 hours long so it was very uncomfortable.

They had memories of some very long days, which began at 2 a.m., and at 4 a.m. there was a briefing on the mission that would last up to an hour. The planes took off at 6 a.m. and those who made it back would often not land until 6 p.m.

Another veteran who returned in 2002 was Lieutenant-General Jerry Johnson, a war ace who vividly remembered the fear and exhilaration of dogfights over Europe's skies. He said: 'We would be flying at 20,000 to 30,000 feet and follow [the Germans] down almost to the ground in these fights. It got your heart pumping and your adrenaline going. You just hoped you wouldn't get shot down.'

Among the countless societies and organisations that still bind Suffolk and the States is the Martlesham Heath Aviation Society, which also celebrates the RAF pilots who flew the night raids. Dating from 1917, Martlesham is Suffolk's oldest airfield and during 1940 a Rhodesian squadron was stationed there, one of whose pilots was Ian Smith, later Prime Minister of Rhodesia. In the same year the first Spitfire landed at Martlesham and, when the No. 85 Squadron arrived, it was led by Squadron Leader Peter Townsend (later Group Captain). A few months later No. 242 Squadron arrived and had as its commanding officer one of the most famous fighter pilots of the Second World War, Douglas Bader. In October 1943 the Americans moved in. Now, when veterans visit the new Martlesham Heath museum, opened jointly by representatives of the RAF and USAAF, they invariably end up in the nearby pub, called The Douglas Bader.

TWO

'You can take the girl out of Ipswich': Suffolk's GI brides

ANYONE VISITING THE RMS *Queen Mary* in her dry dock at Long Beach, California might marvel at the luck of some 13,000 war brides and children who were shipped from Britain to the United States on this luxurious liner, although conditions in 1946, when the voyages began, were very different to those of today. Transporting around 50,000 British women to their new homes across the Atlantic was a logistical nightmare. At the same time there was an overwhelming need to redeploy thousands of American troops back home, but the movement of the wives, fiancées and children of servicemen was to become the largest female mass migration in British history. As East Anglia had one of the highest GI populations in England, many of those who left came from the towns and villages of Suffolk. They were swapping green fields and security for the wide-open spaces of

North America and, in many cases, for nothing more than a promise of marriage, carried through with a youthful and emotional mixture of excitement, anticipation and trepidation.

Evelyn Garrard was one of many Suffolk girls who married GIs and went to the States as a war bride on the *Queen Mary* in 1946. The Garrard family lived in Alderton, near Woodbridge, where Jack and Lilian Garrard ran the local butcher's shop that had been a family business since the 1880s. Evelyn met her future husband in Felixstowe and he told her afterwards that he had taken one look at her and told his friend there and then, 'I'm going to marry that girl.' They were married in Alderton church and the family splashed out on a marquee for the reception, a brave gesture of welcome and approval in war-deprived England.

Evelyn was one of those aboard the *Queen Mary* when she set sail for New York in 1946, together with hundreds of other women and children. Conditions on board were 'frugal, but adequate'. The decoration was austere and there was no on-board entertainment. During the war the original luxury fittings had been removed and exchanged for tiers of bunks and hammocks to facilitate troop movement. Small-calibre guns were fitted, although her main protection in wartime was always her speed. The propulsion machinery produced a massive 160,000 shaft horsepower and gave a speed of over thirty knots. The *Queen Mary*'s war service was second to none as she carried large numbers of troops across different parts of the world. In 1945 she was again refitted to accommodate civilian passengers and her post-war life began.

Every woman aboard the *Queen Mary* had a tale to tell and for most it was their first time away from home. Some had babies and were going out to meet their husbands for the first time in months, some having known them for only a few weeks. Others had married and were going to meet their in-laws with no certainty of a welcome.

After docking Evelyn went by train from New York to California and remembers one girl who travelled with her being dropped off along the way at a small, deserted station 'somewhere in the middle of the US', with not much more than a shack beside the rail tracks. Contrary to her expectations, no one was there to meet her. As the train drew away, leaving the girl alone with her only possessions at her feet, Evelyn often wondered whether she was one of those who got to America only to find that her sweetheart was already married, or had given her a false address.

In truth, many girls barely recognised their new spouses when they met again. Some of them had hardly seen their men out of uniform and when they did they wanted to get back on the boat. For many it was like beginning again with only a surname in common. For those who had scarcely been out of Ipswich, or who came from the remote rural villages, America was a frighteningly large and alien place. Most of what they knew about America came from the movies or *A Bride's Guide to the USA*. This was a leaflet published in 1945 by *Good Housekeeping* magazine, which advised that 'except in the smallest villages, lipstick is expected', and 'most Americans are shy below the surface; they talk to cover it up'.

For Evelyn, though, her journey from Suffolk to California turned out to be a successful and happy time. She arrived in California to a warm welcome and a faithful, honest husband with whom she had a long and happy life – and three children – until he died in 1985. In fact she liked her new life so much that a few years later she persuaded her younger sister, Lilian (known as Paddy), to leave Alderton and join her in California. Paddy went out to join her sister on the *Parthia*. Like Evelyn she swapped Suffolk for the west coast of America and later married a Californian.

In 1950 Jack and Lilian Garrard went to visit their daughters and their families in California but while there Lilian became ill. Fearing that she would lose her sight she sent for her third daughter, Lorna, who flew out to join the family. Amazingly, Lorna too met and fell in love with an American, Jim Andersen, and married him. For the first two years she was homesick for Suffolk but eventually got used to having two homes and now lives with her son close by her older sister, Evelyn.

Over the years the Garrard girls have returned to visit Alderton, and Lorna remembers that on her first visit back to Suffolk nothing seemed to have changed. But gradually a few things did and on a visit to Suffolk in 1980 even the landscape seemed to be different, the trees had grown significantly and there were spaces in her family and her friends' families where people had died. The place that changed least was Alderton Church: 'I remember there was a curtain in the church that looked as if it had been there for a very long time. I don't think it would have survived being moved or taken down for cleaning.' With their three daughters living in America, Jack and Lilian too decided to make California their home, and never returned to Suffolk.

Sixty years on, the *Queen Mary* is paying its own tribute to the GI war brides by mounting a permanent exhibition on board. She made her last transatlantic crossing as a luxury liner in September 1967, when people began to prefer the ease and speed of air travel, after which Cunard sold her to the town of Long Beach. She is now used as a museum, hotel and conference centre.

Not all the women were lucky enough to marry their American serviceman boyfriends, and extraordinary stories have emerged over the years as a result of children trying to find their American fathers. Some babies born to married women whose British husbands were away were simply and quietly added to the existing family, whilst others were born to women whose boyfriends were shipped back to the States before they knew they were pregnant and were not heard from again. (In some cases men simply disappeared overnight as they were repatriated with little or no warning.) When the war ended it had been presumed that the GIs who were in France would return to England to fetch their wives, but in the event they were shipped straight back to America and the women and children told they would have to follow separately. If the woman was pregnant but unmarried it was almost impossible to fulfil the necessary immigration requirements. Later, when the Transatlantic Children's Enterprise (TRACE) was started enquiries poured in from the 'war babies' trying desperately to find their fathers.

Amazing stories have emerged from these years, not least that of Vincent O'Neil of Jamestown, North Dakota who in 1994 discovered that his mother was not, in fact, his real mother. He had been born in Ipswich in 1945 and unofficially adopted two months later by a woman who married an American serviceman stationed at Framlingham.

It transpired that Marianne O'Neil had been living at Martlesham when a young woman named Kate called to collect premiums for the Prudential Insurance Company. Kate was pregnant and was not sure whether the baby belonged to her husband or to an American serviceman. Her husband said he wanted nothing to do with the child either way. Kate and Marianne came to an 'arrangement'. Kate went to her sister's to have the baby, who was born in October 1945 and named Peter Richard. On 14 November Kate handed the baby over to Marianne, who changed his name to Vincent O'Neil. No other formality was entered into, other than a scrap of paper which typed up the bare facts of what had happened and which was signed by both Marianne and Kate. The following year Marianne, by then Mrs Robert O'Neil (having married her American serviceman lodger), took advantage of the relaxation of visa requirements for 'alien spouses and alien children' of American citizens serving aboard. She registered the 'birth' of Vincent at the nearest US embassy and, with a forged paper relating to her own identity, entered America as a war bride. In 1946 Vincent and his English 'mother' left England from the transit base for war brides at Tidworth Camp, Hampshire. She settled first in Minnesota, then North Dakota, and lived in America until her death at the end of 1992.

The discovery of his true identity two years later led Vincent on a long journey from America to Suffolk and to the traumatic discovery that his adoptive mother had at one time been married to the Revd Lionel Foyster. Between 1930 and 1935 the Foysters had lived at the notorious Borley Rectory, a few miles west of Sudbury. As Marianne Foyster she was not only known as 'the most haunted woman in England', through the strange paranormal sightings at the Rectory, but it was thought she might have been implicated in the unlawful killing of the Revd Foyster. Vincent was finally reunited with his birth family and is now one of the world's leading experts on the events surrounding the ghostly sightings, and authenticated poltergeist activity, at Borley Rectory.

The relationship between Suffolk and America did not end with the Second World War. There are still two US Air Force bases in Suffolk, at Mildenhall and Lakenheath, neither of which was used by the Americans during the Second World War, and for over forty years the twin airbases at Woodbridge and Bentwaters were under the control of the USAAF. Hardly surprising, therefore, that the links between the States and Suffolk are inextricable and there is much heart-tugging between people on either side of the Atlantic as families are split across two continents.

One of the many hundreds of Suffolk women who have married American servicemen since the end of the war is Christine Glenn (née Godfrey) who met her future husband at the Airmen's Club at the Bentwaters Air Force Base. Christine writes from Texas: 'I guess I was a GI bride. I always thought that the women who married American servicemen during the Second World War were called GI brides, the rest of us just married Americans.'

Christine worked in the cashier's cage at the club and remembers that she had heard only bad things about the local girls who went out to the base. She had an aunt who talked her into a job there and, once on the base, found that it was nowhere near as bad as she had heard, and the pay was also a lot higher than the Co-op where she had been working on one of the mobile grocery shops:

> I met my husband in November 1968. I had been eyeing him for a number of weeks. When I finally got his attention he didn't stand a chance! I was with some friends at one of the many dances held at the base and we 'just happened' to find ourselves sitting at the table beside him and his friends. He was chatting to one of the girls I was with and they found that they were both from Texas. He asked her out! I couldn't believe it. I'd had my eye on him for ages.

All was not lost because a few weeks later one of the airmen told Christine that his room-mate had a crush on her. She asked who it was and to her delight it sounded like her man. Sure enough, when the airman next arrived at the club he started to talk to her and asked if he could see her the following night. Not being one to waste time, Christine asked, 'How about tonight?'

The airman's name was David Glenn and he was from Tyler, Texas. Christine married him at Bethesda Baptist Church in June 1970. In November that year they moved to Montgomery, Alabama:

> I didn't like Alabama at all. We moved to Dallas in September 1971 and have been in the Dallas area ever since. My husband died in 1997 but I have two adult children in Dallas so I guess I'll stay here because they are not moving to Ipswich!

Not all English brides found a welcome in their new families but Christine's in-laws took her to their hearts and treated her, literally, like one of the family. The biggest problem was that she could not drive. Not all cities then had bus services. If the grocery store, school or doctor's surgery was not within walking distance, women were tied to the house until their men got home in the evenings.

It was sixteen years before Christine 'plucked up the nerve' to get on a plane and return home. In December 1986 she arrived in Suffolk and discovered just how much Ipswich really was 'home':

> I wanted to stand on the Cornhill and yell, 'Hey people, I used to live here – do you remember me? I have missed you more than I ever dreamed I could.' I really looked at the people as I walked through town trying to see if I recognised anyone or to see if they might recognise me. I wanted to stop people and tell them how lucky they are to live in Ipswich and how much I envied them.

Like the Garrard sisters a generation before, three of the Godfrey sisters also made their homes in America. Christine's two sisters – Judy who lives in California, and Elaine who shares a home with Christine just outside Dallas – often meet up and revisit Ipswich together:

> We all head for the travel stop restaurant on the way from the airport for a cream cake or custard tart, to get our holiday started on the right foot. From there on it's the cake shop, fish and chip shop, Woolworth's for pick'n'mix and all the other foods we miss.

In between all these snacks Christine manages to visit her family:

I miss my mother's baking. Cheese scones, sausage rolls and the steak and kidney pudding she used to make in the old copper in the kitchen. If you mention steak and kidney pudding over here, the reaction is 'Yuck, you actually eat kidney?'

Some things, though, are not the same:

I hate that there is a shopping mall in place of Tower Ramparts School. I would love to have been able to go look around all the old classrooms. My other old school buildings are still there, Christchurch School and Smart Street. It used to be such a long walk to school when I was a child, but now I find the distance is not nearly as long as I remembered. Maybe I just enjoy the walk a little more.

When she returns to Dallas, Christine takes all kinds of things with her, including a gallon-size jar of Heinz salad cream, large bags of Tetley teabags, and pounds of Cadbury's Roses chocolates. If she gets desperate in between trips she goes to the British import store in Dallas to stock up:

Last time my brother came to visit he brought a dozen custard tarts with him. Lovely! . . . I guess you can take the girl out of Ipswich, but thank goodness, you will never be able to take Ipswich out of the girl.

Christine misses those family members she left behind in Suffolk and is envious that they can all get together for family occasions. But she has a small Union Jack on her computer at work and the nametag on the desk is a Union Jack with her name on it and Rule Britannia!

Not all marriages, of course, worked out. The culture clash came for the girls who married Hispanic males. Hispanic people are inclined to speak Spanish in the home and if the women did not speak the language they were out in the cold. The families of the men often resented the English women and made it all too clear that their sons had made the wrong choice. The food was different, too. It was very spicy and unfamiliar in the days before curry became England's number one take-away food. It was also a culture in which the man was very much in charge of the house and home. Many of the girls who married Hispanic Americans were quickly divorced.

Homesickness and fear of the unknown also dogged many new brides. Susan Hernandez was born and raised in Ipswich. She married Salvador Hernandez Jnr., a Technical Sergeant in the USAF at RAF Bentwaters, but was filled with doubt and fear even before she left England:

> When I left Ipswich I was only 21 years old, and thought I knew it all! How wrong I was. When the plane left the ground I cried and cried. When I arrived in Texas, I was still crying.

When she got to America the first things she missed were fish and chips, the local pub and Sunday afternoon cricket matches. Like Christine Glenn, she found that not being able to drive was a disadvantage in a car-dominated society and the lack of public transport curbed her independence. Since those early days Susan has acclimatised to life in America but in 1992 the Hernandez family home was destroyed by the F4 tornado that hit the Channelview area on 21 November. Thousands of homes were destroyed and the US President declared it a disaster area.

Whenever Susan comes back to Suffolk the first place she visits is Felixstowe, her 'most favourite place in the world'. Her family still live in Ipswich, Rushmere, Chantry, Gainsborough and Whitton and, although she has had twenty-three happily married years as Mrs Hernandez, there is a corner of her heart that is forever Suffolk.

THREE

Close encounters: the alien invasion of Suffolk

EARLY ON THE morning of 27 December 1980 something extraordinary took place on the edge of Rendlesham Forest, only a few miles from Woodbridge and close to the twin United States Air Force (USAF) bases of Bentwaters and Woodbridge. Patrolmen saw a bright and unusually white light emanating from an object that appeared to hover close to the ground. The object was described as a metal, triangular-shaped box, with a row of blue lights underneath its body and a red pulsing light on top. It hovered for several minutes without touching the ground but as the patrolmen came into its path it glided away through the trees and out of sight. The object was briefly sighted approximately an hour later close to the base perimeter. Immediately afterwards the light seemed to break into five separate white lights, and then disappeared. Then, three star-like objects were seen in the sky, two to the north and one to the south.

The patrolmen quickly returned to base to radio for help. They later reported that they had also seen and communicated with several small aliens, each one about three feet tall with grey skin and a large head. These 'beings', which wore pressure suits but no helmets, were suspended above the ground by shafts of light and were apparently making repairs to the outside of their craft.

This incident was to become known as one of the world's most authenticated and controversial Unidentified Flying Object (UFO) sightings, which has puzzled and intrigued believers and non-believers alike for over twenty years. But had it all been a figment of imagination, or something that could be easily explained by the USAF authorities or their British counterparts? In the absence of logical explanation there could be only one solution: it was a UFO.

If USAF personnel had been the only witnesses to this phenom-enon the story might never have reached the public domain. Governments are notoriously careful when it comes to admitting that UFOs exist at all, never mind that they have been spotted near a major United States military base. The sightings took place in a sensitive part of Suffolk that is only a few miles from Orfordness which in 1915 became the bomb testing site for the Armament Experimental Squadron. In the 1930s this same site was used for top-secret military experiments, including radar, and in the 1950s a series of UFO sightings was reported at USAF bases Bentwaters and Lakenheath, occurring in the same month that scientists at Orfordness tested a secret atomic device.

Just along the coast is Shingle Street, more a dot on a map than a village, but a place wrapped in mystery and conspiracy. In 1942 Shingle Street was evacuated without warning and no official explanation given. There were rumours that at least a hundred badly burned bodies had been washed up on the shore and locals began to talk of a loud explosion out at sea. A cover-up of some sort was suspected and conspiracy theories ran riot. Government files were later released which gave several reasons for the evacuation, including the laying of minefields and weapons' experiments, but rumours persist and the name Shingle Street is synonymous with secrecy and intrigue.

All these coincidences could be considered just coincidences if the 1980 sighting had not occurred close to a vast stockpile of nuclear weapons, and five miles from the Sizewell nuclear power station. This was more than enough for the American government to suppress an alleged UFO incident under the American National Security Act of 1947 and for the British government to cloak it in Her Majesty's Official Secrets Act.

The American association with Bentwaters began in 1942 when the site became part of the 8th Air Force presence in England. The immediate environs comprise isolated beaches and heaths dominated by Corsican pine trees and the yellow flowers of broom and gorse. Here, in 1943, Sutton Heath Airfield (later RAF Woodbridge) was built and it is said that a million pine trees were felled to accommodate one of Britain widest and longest military runways. In 1951 the USAF took over both Bentwaters and Woodbridge, both of which a few years later were to form part of NATO's worldwide network of bases. By the 1980s the twin bases were under the immediate jurisdiction of the Department of Defense in Washington. No wonder, then, that both the USAF and the Ministry of Defence (MOD), which still had nominal responsibility for the bases, were anxious to keep mysterious occurrences under wraps.

For the most part, details of the spectacular events of the days surrounding 27 December were kept secret but word got round that 'something' had happened. Several people in Ipswich reported seeing strange lights in the sky. This could have been coincidence, or mistaken identity, but most of the descriptions gave more or less the same details. The timings were later compared with the times of local aircraft flights, but none matched conclusively, although once it became clear that sightings had taken place over several nights, from 26 to 29 December, it became difficult to establish irrefutable accuracy as to time and place. One witness said he saw the object fly silently over his home in Ipswich, describing it as 'an upturned mushroom glowing phosphorescent'. His dog, whose barking alerted him, became ill the next day and died shortly afterwards.

The day after the UFO 'landing' a forestry worker sought out the crash site. There was damage to the trees and three strange marks on the ground. Later these indentations were said to register abnormally high levels of radiation at all three points.

Over the days in question, an uncorrelated object was recorded on the radar screens at RAF Watton in Norfolk, and several other radar tracking stations in the area picked it up, including one that tracked it crossing the coast off Lowestoft heading for Rendlesham Forest. It emerged later that a few days after the alleged sighting USAF personnel visited all the tracking stations and removed those radar recordings which had allegedly been made during the two days and nights.

One of the first people to hear the UFO rumours was local paranormal investigator, Brenda Butler, contacted by an American friend who was a security officer at Bentwaters. He told Brenda about the 'big light crashing down from the sky into the woods' and together with Jenny Randles and Dot Street she began collecting eye-witness accounts. They would later put all their findings together in a book entitled *Sky Crash*, published in 1984, which put the incident in the public eye for the first time.

As soon as they started asking questions the three came up against a wall of silence from both the MOD and the USAF. It was to be three years before they, and subsequent investigators, received any sort of official confirmation of the UFO (and then only in America under the Freedom of Information Act). During the silent years that followed the sightings, myths developed and flourished, so that it later became difficult to separate fact from fiction.

Somewhat surprisingly this UFO, or at least what was known about it from rumour and hearsay, was not immediately treated seriously by the ufologist fraternity. They seemed sceptical (perhaps because of the talk of small aliens) and needed further convincing that it was not a hoax. The most important similar incident before December 1980 was at Roswell, New Mexico in July 1947 (the Rendlesham incident became known as 'Britain's Roswell'). That, too, occurred near an Air Force base and the Federal authorities mounted a top-secret clean-up operation. Debris, allegedly of alien bodies and their craft, said to have included a visor-type headpiece and what were described as 'alien artefacts', was removed. No such evidence was claimed at Rendlesham, only abnormal concentrations of radiation measured on the site.

However, what made this incident important was the number of high level and apparently credible eye-witnesses.

The *Sky Crash* book brought forward new testimonies. Hundreds of people across Suffolk had seen lights of some description in the skies over three or four nights but given that it was Christmas time, some of these had to be disputed on obvious grounds. There was also a report from the British Astronomical Association that on one of the nights an exceptionally bright meteor, as bright as a full moon, had been seen over southern England.

It became vital for the British ufologists that evidence held by the MOD should be accessed in order to convince the sceptics. A memo had reputedly been written to the MOD by the USAF's Lieutenant-Colonel Charles Halt, to which no answer was received and about which there was no inquiry. The Halt Memo was not officially published in Britain until 2002, although American ufologists examined it some years before.

The memo stated that (1) there was a landing of a small metal craft on the night of 27 December, (2) there was a discovery of excess radiation on the ground, and (3) there was another sighting the following night which Halt himself claimed to have witnessed.

Halt also made a tape of his experience. When it was eventually played, however, it appeared to have been edited, although Halt spoke of chasing the eerie glowing 'saucer-like' object into the forest. It was, he said, able to manoeuvre through trees and was surrounded by light movements that appeared to defy the laws of physics.

In 1997 the Rendlesham UFO controversy surfaced again. Airman First Class Warren, one of the patrolmen who saw the UFO at Rendlesham, decided to put his story into a book. On the night of December 1980, Larry Warren was a nineteen-year-old USAF security policeman on watch, armed with an M16 rifle. He wrote:

> As my mind tried to register what I was looking at, the ball of light exploded in a blinding flash. Shards of light and particles fell onto the fog. Several cops ran into the woods. I couldn't move: I tried to cover my eyes, but it was too late. Now, right in front of me, was a machine occupying the spot where the fog had been.

He also said that he and the other police personnel had been ordered to sign statements contradicting what they had seen and warned to tell no one about it. If they went public, the message was quite simply: 'bullets are cheap'. In their book, *Left at East Gate*, Warren and co-writer Peter Robbins describe their mission to set out the facts and let them speak for themselves. They questioned witnesses, took depositions, visited and revisited the Rendlesham sites, and began pressuring governments on both sides of the Atlantic. In *Left at East Gate* there is a description of the aliens by one of the military personnel:

> They were small, about three to four feet tall and somewhat ghost-like in appearance. They had large heads with catlike black eyes. I could not see other facial features. They were not human at all, but I was not frightened. Each wore very bright, almost silvery clothing. I could not see any life-support devices attached to the entities.

One of the witnesses was Jim Penniston, USAF Technical Sergeant, who was assigned to the 81st Tactical Fighter Wing Security Patrol Squadron at Bentwaters in 1980. In a statement later given to *Omni* magazine, Penniston said that on the night of 26 December he and other personnel reported for guard duty. At around midnight he was despatched to the East Gate at RAF Woodbridge:

> Upon arriving at the East Gate, Staff Sgt Steffans told me that there was a problem out in the woods. I gazed about 300 meters into the distance and saw what appeared to be a fire. My first impression was that we had an aircraft down. I saw orange, red, and bluish types of glowing light, pretty standard with aircraft crashes. I asked Staff Sgt Steffans if he had heard it go down. He told me there had been no sound, that it didn't crash.

Still sure that it was a fallen aircraft, Jim Penniston and two security policemen left the base to investigate. As he got closer it was apparent that it was not an aircraft, though he had no idea what else it could be:

> We entered the tree line and moved in about 20 more metres. There was an object sitting in a clearing. It was emitting mostly white light at that point, very bright. Both [Airman] Burroughs and I had to squint when we looked at it. I found it very strange that there was no sound coming from the object, but the animals around us were in a frenzy. We had wildlife running by us, and lots of birds. Outside that noise, however, there was no other.

Jim Penniston's statement is long and detailed, much of it based on notes he took at the time. Unlike the 'aspirin-shaped' object described by other witnesses he describes it more along the lines of the Halt Memo, triangular in shape, with its main body looking as though it was made of smooth, opaque, black glass. The top was producing a white light, while other lights alternated from grey to blue. Luckily, Penniston had a camera with him: it was standard practice in the prevailing climate of IRA terrorist attacks to take photographs of people on the base perimeters. Knowing that no one was going to believe what he had seen, he took shot after shot of the weird craft, and got within ten feet of it snapping as he went. Much to the frustration of ufologists worldwide, Penniston's photographs were never returned to him. He dropped the films off at the base laboratory for developing and he never got them back. The films, he was told, had not come out. He and all other personnel were also forbidden to speak of the incident or make any public statement on what had happened. He was given six days' leave and lost no time in revisiting the scene. He took plastercasts of the three indentations in the ground, which he believed had been left there by the craft. He initially buried them for safekeeping, suspicious that they might mysteriously 'disappear'.

Over the next few years the UFO story gathered momentum, urged on by local investigators determined to keep up the pressure on the MOD. (In November 2002 a file was finally made available to the British public, which was found to contain a large quantity of correspondence between the MOD and members of the public. Genuine anxiety had been expressed by many people living in Suffolk about the apparent lack of government concern.)

More witness statements were taken and checked out.

Numerous writers and newspaper reporters interviewed local people, and eventually USAF personnel. In no other UFO case anywhere in the world have there been so many credible witnesses. On the first night alone there were some eighty people involved and on the second night an additional thirty, all of them trained military observers. Various reports and allegations continued to filter out from America to England. Each piece of information was vociferously fought over and the courts were employed to invoke the American Freedom of Information Act. Some accounts contained details of an 'alien invasion' and Jim Penniston even agreed to be questioned by a psychologist under hypnosis, during which he said that the beings were 'travellers from our future'. But at no point, then or since, was there any suggestion that the alien intruders were hostile or that they used or suggested violence.

The latest book on the Rendlesham mystery is *You Can't Tell the People*, by Georgina Bruni, in which the author puts forward a convincing case that an incident in the nature of a possible encounter with extraterrestrial beings did occur. Bruni based her research on more than a hundred civilian and military witnesses, some from the MOD, and took her title from the reply given by Baroness Thatcher to Bruni's request for an opinion on UFOs: 'UFOs! You must get your facts right, and you can't tell the people.'

Soon after the book was published in 2000 it became the subject of questions in the House of Lords and since then some seventeen questions have been tabled in an effort to release more information from MOD files. However, the book came in for intense criticism by Larry Warren, co-author of *Left at East Gate*, who claimed that there were 'a staggering 407 problems' with Bruni's book. This only served to fuel the debate.

In order to explain what happened in Rendlesham Forest in 1980 it is the instinct of most healthy sceptics to suggest the involvement of a degree of mass hysteria. So far as we know, UFOs do not land on earth every day, so it is certain that when such a thing occurs it will attract widely differing opinions and speculation. When, in 1983, the story hit the British press, the front page of the *News of the World* screamed 'UFO lands in Suffolk –

and that's official'. The incident was always going to be a magnet for supporters and detractors alike.

There were suggestions that the 'flying saucer' was nothing more than a prank that went too far and was covered up to save embarrassment to the USAF. Others thought it might have been nothing more than a light aircraft. The wife of one of the military officials at the base was told by her husband that she had seen not a flying saucer but a new type of helicopter!

A better-supported theory was that the UFO was in reality no more than flashes from the Orford Ness lighthouse, visible at night from the base. This possibility was explored shortly after the *News of the World* lit the fuse for the nation's ufologists. Ian Ridpath took a camera crew from the BBC's *Breakfast Time* television programme to Rendlesham and set about debunking the UFO theory. He contacted a local forester, who lived within a mile of the alleged sighting and supported the lighthouse theory. Ridpath carried out various experiments with the pulsing beams of the lighthouse and, for many viewers of breakfast television that, together with the exploding meteorite, answered the problem. It was found convenient not to ask the basic question: if the UFO was, in fact, caused by the lighthouse why had the 'mistake' not occurred before?

Had others seen this phenomenon before 1980 and ignored it? If so, why? Also, what of the numerous accounts of electrical devices that faulted in the immediate vicinity? Why were Penniston's films said to be blank, and why did the base laboratory not develop them? And why should there have been numerous, independent reports of animals in various states of frenzy?

When the Rendlesham File was published in 2002, Brenda Butler told the *East Anglian Daily Times* that there had been unexplained lights and images over Rendlesham Forest since the 1600s. The File, she said, contained nothing new: 'The MoD only seemed to get interested in this case because the Americans were involved. There is an awful lot going on down there – more so now than ever.' Brenda maintains that she and her partner Peter Parish still spend many nights in Rendlesham Forest where they see unexplained lights and images.

What did happen in Rendlesham Forest in 1980? Have hundreds of American servicemen made up this incredible story, for reasons best known to themselves, and completely invented not only the physical appearance of a spacecraft but also the stature and physicality of its attendant alien crew? Or was it a cover-up for something more serious, like a malfunctioning weapon, or a terrorist attack?

If, however, the eye-witness accounts are not the product of over-active imaginations, or government cover-ups, we are left with the possibility that in 1980 creatures from outer space visited Suffolk on several consecutive nights. They came, according to Jim Penniston under hypnosis, 'because their world is not like ours. It is darker, very polluted and much colder.' He said that they told him that they were people from the future and that their world had serious problems and difficulties with reproduction. Is this a warning of things to come on earth – a friendly nod from futurist humans returning in a Dr Who Tardis?

Trying to unravel the story of Suffolk's UFO is like being blown along Shingle Street by a north-easterly wind: first veering one way, thinking it impossible that so many people could be wrong about such an extraordinary series of incidents; then the other, with a considered and logical explanation presented coolly, with dismissive confidence, each witness statement debunked in turn. Can we easily believe that beings from another planet, and another time, embarked on space travel from somewhere in the universe and landed purely by chance in Rendlesham Forest? Then read again the first-hand accounts of what hundreds of people saw in the skies over Suffolk and we must wonder how it might be possible for so many to fabricate such stories and maintain their consistency under sustained questioning over twenty years.

European artists as far back as the fifteenth century recorded strange objects in the sky. In a painting by Filippo Lippi (1406–69) a man and a dog look up at a saucer-shaped object in the sky, while another painting of 1429 shows a number of dark, elongated 'clouds' in what is said to be a 'real event' in Rome in the second half of the fourth century AD.

More recently a correspondent to the *East Anglian Daily Times* wrote: 'Upon being confronted by a similar recurring [UFO] situation in 1990, the Belgian Air Force attempted to intercept numerous low-level encounters before the unknown craft left the area (the aircraft radar tapes were published).' The Belgian authorities undertook an investigation and admitted there was no conventional explanation.

But, if these alien intruders came to Suffolk . . . who were they? What did they want . . . and did they get what they came for? And . . . will they one day return?

FOUR

Haunted Suffolk

MAYBE IT IS because total darkness still exists in the Suffolk country-side at night, but walking down a quiet country lane on a pitch-black night heightens the senses and fuels the imagination. Mass murderers lurk behind every tree and the screech of a vixen in the still and silent night can chill the blood of even the most seasoned and experienced country dweller. No wonder that ghost and mystery stories abound in Suffolk folklore, such that legends of a ferocious black dog could keep people in their houses at night while the smugglers landed their booty and plied their trade. There are numerous versions of 'Black Shuck', a fierce black hound that lurked in hidden dens, whose white, flashing teeth would scare almost anyone. Tales of the ghost of the notorious 'Black Toby' of Blythburgh are told to this day. Coaches driven by headless men with headless horses were seen at night on Suffolk roads, and God-fearing persons stayed at home for fear of witnessing such apparitions and the ill luck that would follow.

The Black Dog of Bungay remains one of the most persistent of these stories and concerns the apparition of the Devil in the disguise of a black dog in St Mary's Church on 4 August 1577. On that Sunday a terrifying storm, with torrential rain, struck the town. The congregation heard the rain and thunder shaking the building. Suddenly a flash of lightning rent the stones. According to a pamphlet published by Abraham Fleming, there was 'darkness, rain, hail, thunder and lightning and was never seen the like.'

During this storm the people saw a black dog enter the church, his mouth snarling, showing white and hideously sharp fangs. 'A strange and terrible wunder wrought very late in the parish church of Bungay' was described by Abraham Fleming's pamphlet, which carried Mr Fleming's drawing of the hound. This horrifying creature caused the townspeople to kneel in fear, praying for mercy. Those who witnessed the event confirmed that a great black Hound of Hell had appeared in their midst and began rampaging around the church, attacking the congregation with its teeth and claws. An old verse records:

All down the church in midst of fire
The hellish monster flew;
And passing onward to the choir
He many people slew.

As the storm raged the church tower was struck by lightning, the clock broke in thousands of pieces and the churchwarden's account book records that two men in the belfry were killed. In a sixteenth-century tract the Black Dog was said to have 'wrung the necks of them bothe at one instant clene backward insomuch that, even at a moment where they kneeled, they straungely died'. Another unfortunate man survived the attack, but was said to have shrivelled up like a piece of leather scorched in a hot fire.

There had long been a belief that satanic black hounds roamed the Bungay area and that the disasters experienced were the work of the Devil. Those who survived considered themselves lucky, but warned – warned of what is not exactly clear, but such was the power of the story that the Black Dog is incorporated into the town's coat of arms where it is shown running along a flash of lightning. The name lives on in the Black Dog Running Club,

Black Dog Marathon, Black Dog Antiques and 'Black Dogs', the name of the Bungay Town Football Club.

Having taken its retribution on the people of Bungay, the Black Dog moved on to Blythburgh where it seared the north door of Holy Trinity Church with scorch marks caused, so the legend says, when the ferocious creature found the door closed. It terrorised the congregation of Blythburgh before disappearing back to Hell, from where it was thought to have come. There, too, a flash of lightning struck the spire and sent tons of masonry crashing through the roof and a man and a boy were killed. The marks on the door were considered to be those of the Devil incarnate and people spoke of the sulphurous smell that remained in the air long after the Black Dog had left.

Over the years stories of the Black Dog – or Shuck – have refused to die and recently a lecturer at University College, Northampton decided to compile a database of such sightings in an attempt to analyse these apparitions and investigate claims of the paranormal. Although in the late sixteenth century superstitious beliefs were at an all-time high it is likely that an incident of some kind did occur both at Bungay and Blythburgh. Storms of such intensity are by no means rare and dogs are commonly 'freaked' by thunder and lightning. However, whether or not this was a satanic dog sent by the Devil or someone's pet possessed of evil is still open to question. As recently as the 1940s a similar apparition was witnessed by an American airman who, with his wife, had rented a hut on the edge of Walberswick Marsh for his off-duty periods. One night there was a bad storm, similar to that of 1577. Lightning tore across the skies and thunder shook the earth. The couple thought they heard a scratching noise at the door, followed by a series of thuds, and they tried to see out of the window. The rain was pounding against the glass but they both saw what they thought was a huge black dog hurling itself against the wall of the hut. For hours the thudding and scratching carried on. The couple were terrified and piled furniture against the door. But in the morning there was not a single mark on the door and no prints in the ground.

Not all of these Black Dogs are said to have caused actual harm.

Some, like the Galleytrot – as the Black Dog is sometimes called in Suffolk – of Leiston just pads silently about the churchyard.

No future investigation will be made into the Black Beast of Fordham, however, a mysterious apparition that was reported to be haunting the villages around Newmarket, early in 2002. This Black Beast, which only appeared at night, was said to be the size of a Shetland pony and 'as black as the night'. Some villagers said it had 'red glowing eyes as big as saucers'. A few days after these reports found their way into the newspaper the local dog warden braved the lonely and deserted village lanes and tracked down this Black Beast, but found it to be anything but fierce. It was a half-blind, cross-collie dog named Solo which was either lost or had been abandoned. No less vivid imagination was needed to fuel the tales of the Black Dogs of Bungay and Blythburgh. These sound far-fetched to the modern ear, but there is no reason to dispute that an event of some kind took place in 1577 and that it deeply affected those who saw it.

A story of mystery and intrigue that has also stirred people's imagination is that of the Wild Man of Orford, the merman hauled out of the sea by frightened fisherman who caught him in their nets. A Cistercian monk, Ralph of Coggeshall, recorded the event in 1200, saying that it had taken place some forty years earlier. He wrote in his *Chronicon Anglicanum* that in the time of Henry II, when Bartholomew de Glanville was in charge at Orford Castle:

> some fishermen, fishing in the sea there, caught in their nets a wild man. He was naked and was like a man in all his members, covered with hair and with a long, shaggy beard. He eagerly ate whatever was brought to him but if it was raw he pressed it between his hands until all the juice was expelled. He would not talk, even when tortured and hung up by his feet.

It took three men to haul the Wild Man into the boat. They had never seen such a creature and at first thought it was a seal. After a battle to control his flailing arms and legs the men finally subdued him and he lay, bound by ropes, on the bottom of the boat, panting heavily and taking gulps of air like a landed fish. A message was sent to

Bartholomew de Glanville that a prisoner had been caught and instructions were received that he should be taken to the dungeons.

The Wild Man was observed to have webbed hands and feet and, although he showed distress, no human words were discernible and he made only whimpering noises. The guards put him in leg-irons and then left him in the dark where, finally, he curled up and slept. The following morning, and every morning thereafter, the guard took food to him but he never spoke.

Eventually Bartholomew de Glanville became tired of his prisoner and ordered that unless he answered his questions he should be tortured. Despite being hung up by his feet the Wild Man did not – or could not – answer their questions. Then the chaplain was sent to the dungeons, to see what he could do. The chaplain made the sign of the cross over the captive, but he neither bent his knee nor showed by any other means that he understood the Christian sign. Certain then that this was a manifestation of the Devil, the chaplain had the merman tortured again. They strung him up and lit a fire under him until his long hair singed. Then they saw that his skin was not like human skin, but made of green, overlapping scales. They began to hit him, trying to make him talk. But only a gurgling sound came from the throat of the Wild Man and tears flowed from his bewildered eyes. Unmoved, the chaplain ordered that he be cut down and returned to his chains and leg-irons where they left him, hurt and shivering in his dark and miserable prison. He licked his wounds as best he could and tried to cover the scorched scales on his body where the hair had been burnt away.

Gradually Bartholomew de Glanville's interest in the merman waned. In spite of dire warnings from his chaplain he decided that the creature was harmless and gave orders that the Wild Man be allowed down to the shore to where the local fisherman worked. They hung their nets across the harbour entrance and unshackled him so that he could go into the water. For a moment the Wild Man hesitated, unused to the light and his legs being free. He raised his arms up towards the sky and spread out his webbed hands so that they caught a spray of salt water as the sea lapped against the nets, which had been set to prevent his escape. The fishermen watched in disbelief as their charge ran down the shore and slid into the water. In seconds he was gone, diving down to the harbour bottom and underneath the nets to the safety of the open sea.

For several hours the fishermen kept watch on the harbour thinking it impossible that the merman would not have to surface for air. They scanned the horizon until the light was gone, but the sea had reclaimed the Wild Man of Orford and he was never seen again. The chaplain was never able to explain where the creature came from but told everyone that it had drowned and was no longer to be feared. But although it had initially frightened the fishermen, it had never harmed anyone. Quite the contrary, the men at the castle had shamefully maltreated the merman.

Several interpretations can be put on the story but the description of the Wild Man of Orford is similar to other such sightings around the world. Some think that these creatures were the inspiration for the Green Men carved on churches and cathedrals across the kingdom. The carvings are of foliage faces that embody long-held myths and legends of divine help, associated with trees and physical and spiritual regeneration. Wild Men also represented those living on the fringes of society and are thought to have existed in woods and forests. They were outlaws, but represented natural forces believed to be beyond human consciousness. These Green Men are also known as Wild Men, or Woodwoses, and in Suffolk the Green Man is still used as a pub name at Newmarket, Tunstall and Woodbridge.

Carvings of the Green Man – or Woodwose – are found at nearly forty churches in the county, from Clare to Dennington and from Metfield to Nayland. At Norton he is seen wielding a club in combat with a lion, and at St Mary's, Cratfield a grinning dragon is confronted by a woodwose who bears a shield and club. In Victorian times moulds of a version of the Green Man were made in the thousands and appear on buildings throughout the county, in a frieze for instance at Kentwell Hall and on a spandrel in a cottage at Tolly Cobbold's Brewery in Ipswich.

If the Black Dog, the Wild Man and the Green Man are manifestations of forces beyond man's comprehension they are at least partially understood. Ghosts are another matter altogether. By their nature ghosts are invisible for most of the time and are thought to be spectres of persons now dead, each a disembodied spirit which revisits places where he or she lived when alive. One such is Black Toby who adds to the mystery and intrigue of the tidal marsh-lands around Blythburgh.

Tobias Gill, known as Black Toby, was a negro drummer in Suffolk's 4th Regiment of Dragoons, commanded by Sir Robert Rich. In 1748 the signing of the Treaty of Aix-la-Chapelle ended the war of the Austrian succession and two years later, in 1750, Sir Robert brought the men who had fought in that war back to Blythburgh. Like most Dragoons, Black Toby liked his drink but because of his immense strength could do significant damage with his mighty fists. Most of the men in the regiment gave him a wide berth, but not because of the colour of his skin. The regiment had travelled and fought in too many countries to let a man's colour be counted against him. He was feared both by his fellow Dragoons and by the locals who drank in the public houses frequented by the regiment because of his temper and inability to hold his drink. Black Toby was easily annoyed and would often get into a fight over nothing more than a look or a casual comment and could break another man's jaw with one blow.

For all his loutish behaviour, Black Toby was popular with the local women. He was well over six feet tall and in his Dragoon uniform must have been an impressive sight. When sober he was a very different man and had an easy charm that attracted female company. Gradually, though, his reputation went before him and he was banned from the Blythburgh pubs and had to go further afield. One night, in the summer of 1750, Black Toby was making his way back to camp across the heath where he met Ann Blakemore, a Walberswick serving girl on her way home. She knew Black Toby and tried to hurry past him, but he had been drinking heavily and was angered that she would not speak to him.

No one knows exactly what happened, but the next morning Ann was found dead and Black Toby lay next to her still in a drunken stupor. He was arrested and taken to Bury St Edmunds for trial, where he was found guilty of her murder. Although he admitted being drunk he denied emphatically that he had either murdered or raped Ann and protested his innocence throughout.

Black Toby was sentenced to death and returned to Blythburgh where he was taken to the crossroads and hanged in chains on the gallows. Afterwards his body was taken to the spot on the heath where the murder had taken place and put in a gibbet. There it remained until the weather, and the birds and beasts of the heath, left only his bones.

The considerable doubt surrounding Black Toby's guilt is shown by tales that his ghost was seen walking across the heath, manifesting itself to walkers who dared to go near the spot where the gibbet had stood. He was punished for a crime that he said he did not commit and many people believed that he was blamed because of his reputation. No marks were found on Ann's body and there were no signs of a struggle, leaving many to conclude that she had simply died of fright after being confronted with a drunken Black Toby on a moonless night.

Black Toby's ghost is still said to stalk the path from Blythburgh to Walberswick and his restless spirit to roam that part of the estuary known today as Toby's Walks.

Sometimes ghosts manifest themselves for no particular reason. One such is the spirit of a seventeenth-century nun called Penelope who is said to haunt the Elizabethan mansion of Coldham Hall in Stanningfield, near Bury St Edmunds. Sister Penelope was a member of the Rokewood family, who lived at Coldham Hall for several generations after Sir Robert Rokewood built it in 1575. The family stayed faithful to their Catholic beliefs after the Reformation made Protestantism the national religion and Catholics a persecuted minority. One of the Rokewoods, Ambrose, was executed at Tyburn in 1605 for his part in the Gunpowder Plot, although none of this seems to have anything to do with Sister Penelope. She spent her summer holidays peacefully and happily with her family, away from her convent. Several 'authenticated' sightings have been made of her revisiting the Rokewood seat, apparently just for the fun of it.

One of Bury St Edmunds's most famous ghosts is also a nun,

known as The Grey Lady. Called Maude Carew, she was accused of involvement in a plot to assassinate the Duke of Gloucester, brother of Henry VI, who died in 1447 at St Saviour's Hospital, Bury St Edmunds. Maude is said to have poisoned the duke and then herself but, perhaps because like Black Toby she was unjustly accused, her spirit returns at precisely eleven o'clock on the anniversary of her death. To the frustration of ghost-watchers she appears in different places throughout the town, including the ruins of the old Abbey and the Cathedral precincts.

Anyone who thinks that ghosts are an ancient phenomenon, witnessed only by the excited and superstitious people of past ages, would be advised to stay away from the fifteenth-century Ancient House in the centre of Ipswich. Because this is, literally, an ancient house there are many stories of ghosts and mysteries asso-ciated with its 500 year history. But the most recent haunting took place for the first time in the spring of 1997 in that part of the old house that was then a shop, called Lakeland Plastics.

What was at first thought to be a prank began on 14 February when the shop had been decorated with flowers to celebrate St Valentine's Day. The next morning the staff discovered some flowers had been moved, taken out of the vases and placed on the doormat. Although it was dismissed as a joke, it did seem strange that whoever had done it would have needed a key. There was no one in the room when they unlocked the door that morning and, it was noted, whoever had rearranged the flowers had taken considerable trouble over it.

The next occasion was when the shop was decorated for Mothering Sunday, but this time the flowers were removed twice. First they were taken from the vases and later put back in their original arrangement. Other, more sinister, events began to occur. One woman lost her car-park ticket, only for it to reappear the foll-owing day. The same thing happened with a key, which disapp-eared from a cupboard but reappeared. A woman was locked in the cellar. Another saw a vase fall off a window ledge for no apparent reason. Bottles would disappear then reappear and more than once staff members felt as though they had been touched on the shoulder but found no one standing behind them.

Understandably, the staff began to get jittery and the manager decided to call in a medium, before the employees left to look for safer employment. It took no time at all for the medium to decide that the Ancient House, sometimes known by its old name Sparrowe House, was indeed haunted. The name 'Lakeland' kept occurring to her but she thought it was insignificant, since that was the name of the shop.

The story had by this time reached the local newspaper and the Ipswich *Star* ran the story, the result of which was that a curious coincidence was uncovered. Lakeland – or Lackland – was found to be the surname of an Ipswich woman who was burned as a witch in 1644.

Mother Lackland was a victim of the murderous and sadistic Matthew Hopkins, the Witchfinder General, who roamed Suffolk between 1644 and 1647 looking for supposed witches to torture and put to death. The son of a Puritan minister, he practised unsuccessfully as a lawyer in Ipswich before embarking on his 'mission'. Many and horrific are the tales associated with this psychotic, power-crazed murderer whose ways and means of getting women to confess to witchcraft were simple. He would pick on a girl or woman who was then stripped and searched for signs of the Devil. Then they would be tortured into confession by being deprived of sleep and subjected to physical and emotional abuse for days and nights on end. Mother Lackland was one such victim, who confessed that she had been a 'Professor of Religion' for many years and had made a covenant with the Devil. He, in return, had given her three imps in the shape of two little dogs and a mole to use in her trade. She bewitched her husband, who subsequently died, and then went on to do the same to a Mr Lawrence and his child, who also died.

Mother Lackland made a series of 'confessions' at the Ipswich Summer Assizes before the fanatical Witchfinder General and was duly found guilty and burned at the stake. No wonder, then, that Mother Lackland should return to haunt Ipswich, but why the Ancient House? Had the coincidental name of Lakeland brought her back from the dead, and if so, why? Or perhaps the whole episode was an elaborate hoax and publicity stunt?

The solution seemed to lie with the Royalist supporter, William Sparrowe, who once owned the Ancient House and held a banquet there for the restored King Charles II in 1660. Following the publicity about the ghost of Mother Lackland a local historian added a few facts to her story that led him to think that she might have been a Royalist supporter who was tried and convicted on the false, but more popular, charge of witchcraft. Peter Jennings, author of *Supernatural Ipswich*, discovered that Mary and John Lackland lived close to Sparrowe House where, in 1801, a secret room was found and was claimed to have been a hiding place for wanted Royalists. Even King Charles himself might have used the room, which had been sealed for over 150 years. (After the Restoration the then occupant, Robert Sparrowe, adorned the front of Sparrowe House with the coat of arms of Charles II.)

Were Mary and John both Royalist agents, in an intensely pro-Puritan Ipswich? Other men and women were later proved to have been condemned and executed as witches when in fact they had been punished for supporting the king after being betrayed by Puritan spies.

Mary Lackland, convicted of witchcraft, was burned on Cornhill. Had the name Lakeland brought her back, 350 years later, to clear her own name? Shortly after the Royalist connections were made the Lakeland ghost ceased its activities. The coat of arms of Charles II, set into the plaster of the house by the Sparrowe family, can still be seen on the Ancient House in Ipswich.

FIVE

Suffolk daughters

WHO QUALIFIES AS a daughter of Suffolk? Must she have been born here, lived and died here? If so, there are millions of Suffolk daughters. Some of the more famous are mentioned elsewhere in this book, but there are many others whose connections with the county touched or influenced their contemporaries beyond the norm. Suffolk has always been a magnet for writers and artists who are eager to forsake the rat race in favour of the rural idyll and take inspiration from the beautiful East Anglian skies. Until the latter half of the twentieth century this included more men than women, but among the latter was the child-prodigy artist Margaret Scott Somerville. Known as Peggy, she lived and worked in Suffolk from the age of thirteen until her death in 1975.

Peggy Somerville (1918–75) was born into a large and artistic family and had her first solo exhibition at the age of ten, Sir John Lavery expressing himself 'completely mystified by the extraordinary genius of the little girl in the handling of oils, water colours and crayons'. Due to her father's determination that his daughter's talent should remain untutored, Peggy had not had a single art lesson. All one hundred pictures on display were sold and more requested. 'I see the picture in my mind and then just paint it,' explained the young Peggy.

However, a year later at a second exhibition, the art historian and critic R. H. Wilenski wrote disparagingly in the *Evening Standard*, referring to her method as 'splodgy':

> Everyone should go to the exhibition of fifty landscapes in oil by Peggy Somerville, aged eleven . . . because this exhibition should deal the death-blow to a degraded form of pseudo-impressionism that abounds in adult shows . . . I have been convinced that this sort of picture is not art, but child's play, and now Peggy Somerville, who is really a child, has appeared to prove it. The pictures in this show are painted in the 'splodgy' technique.

In 1931 the family moved to Suffolk and during the Second World War Peggy opted to join the Women's Land Army. When demobbed in 1945 she returned with her widowed mother to Suffolk and to painting. After living for a while at her brother Stuart's home, Newbourne Hall, a dilapidated Tudor mansion on the peninsula that lies between the rivers Orwell and Deben, she eventually moved to Westleton and then to Middleton, where she dutifully nursed her elderly mother in relative obscurity.

Peggy died of cancer aged fifty-seven only a short time after the mother for whom she had cared so devotedly. Although she exhibited all over the county on numerous occasions, and during the 1970s had solo exhibitions at her brother's gallery in Saxmundham, both the art and the artist disappeared from the wider public view. However, after her death her sister discovered a cache of drawings, watercolours and pastels, which showed that the former child prodigy might have been out of sight but art had never been out of her mind. She still viewed the world, and in particular her beloved Suffolk, with vibrant, colourful and vivacious vision.

Other Suffolk daughters are perhaps better described as heroines and their stories are numerous and diverse. Boudicca, Margaret Catchpole, Julia Cavendish and the Garretts of Snape Maltings are dealt with in other chapters, but one woman who made Suffolk her home for some seventy years defies the ordinary categories. Lady Evelyn Barbara Balfour (1898–1990), fourth daughter of the 2nd Earl Balfour, and niece of the Conservative prime minister, Arthur Balfour, was a novelist, jazz musician and amateur dramatist, sailor and pilot, and played an active role in the 'tithe war' of the 1930s. She was also a farmer, who trained Land Girls in the First World War, and an internationally known exponent of organic farming and the author of *The Living Soil*, the definitive work on the subject. She set up the Haughley Research Farms, the only farm-scale experiment of its kind, and in 1943 founded the Soil Association, which has gone on to become the most respected mouthpiece for organic agriculture in the world.

Lady Eve was born in London and from an early age wanted to farm. When she was seventeen she went to Reading University, gaining a diploma in agriculture – one of the first women to do so. Together with her sister Lady Mary, Eve went to Monmouthshire in 1918 to run a fifty-acre farm near Newport, under the jurisdiction of the Board of Agriculture. As a result of four years of war, farming was just then enjoying one of its brief spells of profitability. Farmers were seeing rising prices for their output, positive attention from government and the appreciation of a grateful nation. There were guaranteed minimum prices for wheat and despite the appalling lack of resources and awful weather that prevailed over the 1918 harvest, British farmers kept the nation fed.

With men away on active service the Women's Land Army (WLA) took over much of the farm work. Although hostilities ceased in November 1918 the need to provide food was ever more urgent, and as four million men were demobilised and swelled the home population the role of the WLA became imperative. Lady Eve's farm was handed over to the Women's War Agricultural Committee and she began training Land Girls. But by the end of 1919 the need had diminished and Eve's job came to an end both on the farm and with the WLA. She and Mary dreamed of making their childhood ambition of farming on their own account a reality and applied for particulars of farms for rent. She asked for farms in Sussex, but received particulars of farms for sale in Suffolk. Eve had never been to Suffolk but when she saw New Bells Farm in Haughley for the first time she knew it was what she wanted. After some help from her father the farm was purchased and Eve was to live in Suffolk for the next seventy years.

During the 1920s and 1930s farming fortunes took a nosedive but somehow Lady Eve and her sister kept the farm going, often with help from extracurricular activities. She and a few friends formed a jazz band and began playing at the Great White Horse Hotel in Ipswich on Saturday nights. Because of the hotel's connection with Charles Dickens, they called themselves the Pickwick Dance Club, and by popular request were soon engaged to play at other venues.

A year or two later Lady Eve and her lifelong friend, Beb Hearnden, began to co-write detective novels. *The Paper Chase*, by 'Hearnden Balfour', was the first to be published and was followed by *Enterprising Burglar* and others. The novels proved successful and were also published in America.

At the same time Lady Eve became involved in the bitter and complicated dispute between the Established Church and local farmers – the tithe war. She took part in protests across Suffolk and in 1933 her farm at Haughley suffered raids by a company appointed as bailiff to retrieve goods worth unpaid tithe.

It was in 1939, at New Bells Farm, that the world-famous experiments, which compared organic and inorganic methods of farming, were started. Lady Eve's interest had been stimulated by the discovery that compost-grown vegetables in a mainly lacto-vegetarian diet could cure her recurring colds and rheumatism. She read Lord Lymington's *Famine in England*, which questioned the sustainability of orthodox agriculture. It changed the direction of her farming life. Lymington's idea fired her imagination and by the early 1940s she had enough material for a book. In the Introduction to *The Living Soil and the Haughley Experiment*, Lady Eve wrote:

> In this book I have attempted something which my friends tell me cannot be done. I have tried to write for both the specialist and the layman. If I have failed, if what I have written proves to be unintelligible and boring to the layman, and at the same time trite and

superficial to the specialist, I shall be unable to plead that I was not warned, but my only alternative was not to write at all – a depressing one for the would-be author suffering from the belief that he has something important to say.

The book proved to be neither boring nor trite, as it had immediate and enduring success and is, today, considered a classic of its kind. The concept of organic was then in its infancy and derided by the agricultural establishment. She was once accused of being a 'crank', at which she laughed heartily and said she was like a car crank 'which got things going'.

During the Second World War Lady Eve employed Land Girls at New Bells Farm with extra seasonal help at threshing time. One of them later wrote:

> In the Haughley-Old Newton area one farmer, Mr Arthur Stearn, was the owner of the threshing tackle that went round all the farms in turn. His men, of course, worked the machinery and the farmer's men dealt with the corn – incidentally I was always put with the chaff bags. Lady Eve always went and had a friendly word with the foreman.

Unfortunately some of the experiments carried out at New Bells Farm were less than enthusiastically embraced: 'Lady Eve had deliveries of sewerage sent up from Stowmarket, to put on the land in the spring, and the stench around the countryside was absolutely appalling!'

In 1945 the Soil Association was formed with the stated aims of bringing together all those working for a fuller understanding of the vital relationship between soil, plant, animal and man. It was also to initiate, co-ordinate and assist research and collect and distribute the knowledge gained, so creating a body of informed opinion. Lady Eve wanted the Association to stress the positive points of organic husbandry, not to simply attack conventional methods. After the war ended she took her message worldwide, making extensive lecture tours across Europe, America and Australia on behalf of the Association.

In 1963 she moved to Theberton and although she did not officially retire for another twenty years she had more time to cultivate her large garden and two greenhouses. In 1989 she suffered a stroke, on the same day that an invitation arrived from the prime minister, Margaret Thatcher, asking her to join a group of ecologists in Downing Street. She was unable to go but was awarded the OBE in 1990, though she was once again too ill to travel to London to collect it. Her niece, Margaret Folarin, said that Eve was thrilled to get the honour, but the family thought that it was sad that she had not got it earlier. Lady Eve died in 1990, at the age of ninety-one.

In 2001 the Ipswich-based theatre company Eastern Angles put on a musical, by Ivan Cutting and Pat Whymark, about the turbulent years of the tithe war. One of the characters in *Tithe War!* was 'Lady Eve Balfour' and in the audience at Saxmundham were Margaret Folarin and her sister, Frances Whitfield. Frances said afterwards that she had been pleased to see the character of her aunt play the flute as well as the saxophone, since that was the instrument that her family most associated with her.

Lady Eve is remembered with admiration and affection, but one of the least popular daughters of Suffolk is surely Mrs Wallis Simpson, the American socialite who almost brought about the downfall of the British monarchy and took as her third husband the uncrowned Edward VIII. It was to Suffolk that she came, at the end of the Abdication Crisis in 1936, and it was at Ipswich Assizes that she made history, but she was not a welcome visitor.

The feeling of dislike was mutual: Wallis hated Beach House, the sprawling, two-storey residence, where she was to live for six weeks in 1936 in order to establish the residential qualification required for the divorce that would allow her to marry King Edward. The six-bedroomed house, situated in Undercliff Road East, was 'home' to Wallis and two companions, though as she wrote in her autobiography: 'My first impression of the little house in Felixstowe was dismaying. It was tiny, there was barely room for the three of us, plus a cook and a maid, to squeeze into it.'

Bessie Wallis Warfield was born in Baltimore, USA, in 1896. After her first marriage ended, she married Ernest Simpson in 1928 and they moved to London. She rapidly established herself as a hostess and through contacts at the American Embassy became friendly with Thelma Furness, who at the time was married but involved with Prince Edward, the future king.

Soon after he met the Simpsons the Prince, thirty-six and single, invited them to a Palace function. The relationship between Wallis and Edward was initiated and, unknown to the British public, began to flourish. Due to an astonishing gentleman's agreement with British newspaper owners, inconceivable today, no whiff of the impending scandal leaked out. When Edward became king in January 1936 the Prime Minister suggested Wallis should 'steal quietly away'. The situation came to a head towards the end of the year when, after protracted negotiations, it became clear that for any number of reasons the new and as yet uncrowned king could not marry a twice-divorced American and keep the throne. In his abdication speech, made over the radio, the king told his subjects in one of the best-remembered sentences of the twentieth century: 'You must believe me when I tell you that I have found it impossible to carry the heavy burden of responsibility and to discharge my duty as King as I would wish to do, without the help and support of the woman I love.' By the time this speech was made Wallis Simpson had obtained her divorce at a seventeen-minute court hearing on 17 October 1936, in what is now County Hall, Ipswich.

To a woman used to more grandiose surroundings, in the company of princes and the elite of European aristocracy, out-of-season Felixstowe was found wanting. Beach House was secluded, tucked away behind a high, red-brick wall, and from the road was almost invisible. All she had to look at was a view of the grey, cold and unchanging October sea, as she sat for weeks in this draughty house in a quiet Suffolk seaside town. It did nothing to lift her depression over the situation in which she found herself. She wrote: 'The only sounds were the melancholy boom of the sea breaking on the deserted beach and the rustling of the wind around the shuttered cottages. No hint of distant concern penetrated Felixstowe.'

Edward visited her there frequently. He arrived in a small red aircraft (the first monarch to travel by air), which would land on open fields to the east of the seafront, or at Ipswich, and would travel to Felixstowe incognito. When he could not get to Suffolk he would telephone or write and Wallis would walk down into the town to pick up the mail and newspapers. Sometimes she walked on the beach with her little dog, Slipper, and was dismayed at how little attention was paid to her. 'Not a head turned,' she wrote.

In Ipswich a decree nisi was granted, which meant that the decree absolute was another six months away. If the judge believed that the plaintiff was already involved with another man, the divorce would not be forthcoming. The sight of the courtroom portrait of the new (as yet uncrowned) king troubled the presiding judge, said afterwards to have been 'uncomfortable' about events. The hoped-for quiet end to the Simpson marriage turned into a near-riot as the press finally tracked her down.

After the hearing Wallis was whisked away at high speed in a waiting car by her counsel, Norman Birkett, England's most celebrated and flamboyant barrister. She had to crouch down on the floor of her car to avoid the cameras; there was, however, nothing in any of the British newspapers the following morning (although the matter was freely reported in America). The press silence was still unbroken. It was not until 2 December that the first comment appeared in a leading article in the *Yorkshire Post*. Then the floodgates opened.

The following May, Wallis's divorce became absolute and in June she married Edward, HRH the Duke of Windsor, who at his abdication had been replaced by his brother as George VI.

In 1988 Beach House was sold. Plans to knock it down and develop the site were announced and vehemently opposed by conservationists and local historians. But the Council rejected the 'Costa del Sol' style block of flats and the house fell into rack and ruin. In 1993 vandals started a fire inside and later that year Beach House was demolished, with the sanction of the Felixstowe Society. It was taken apart brick by brick, its fireplaces, doors and other features sold at auction. There were protests from residents and historians, but the site was developed and now has only a commemorative plaque to record the momentous events of 1936.

If ever two women could be said to be as different as chalk and cheese, Wallis Simpson and Lady Ryder of Warsaw (1923–2000) might be good candidates. Margaret Susan Ryder, known always as Sue, was born in Yorkshire but came to Suffolk as a child in the 1930s when the family moved to Little Thurlow, near Bury St Edmunds. Until the age of ten, her socially conscious mother, Mabel, taught Sue at home, after which she was sent to the exclusive Kent boarding school Benenden. She was sixteen when the war broke out and she offered her services as a volunteer nurse. In due course she decided to join the all-female voluntary corps the FANY (First Aid Nursing Yeomanry), where she was seconded to work for the SOE (Special Operations Executive).

The SOE was specially formed in July 1940 in accordance with a War Cabinet memorandum for the purpose of 'co-ordinating all action by way of subversion and sabotage against the enemy overseas'. The volunteer nurses worked closely with the SOE, using FANY as a cover for their covert work. SOE members attended saboteur schools where they were trained to run spying and resistance operations behind enemy lines. It was highly secret and extremely dangerous work and, after her secondment to SOE, Sue was required to sign the Official Secrets Act.

She began her new posting, briefly, with the Czech Section, but then became attached to the Polish Section. She worked at preparing and despatching Polish agents (whom she called 'Bods') and in the course of her SOE career three hundred agents passed through her hands. She was impressed by the courage of the men and women embarking on such dangerous missions: 'They went into it in cold blood, of their own choice. They were fighting for us and they didn't have to do it. The fact that they faced what they did, completely aware of what lay ahead, would have an appeal to anyone.' In later years Sue Ryder was reluctant to talk about her SOE years, believing that her oath of secrecy did not end with the war.

In 1945 Sue was with relief units caring for the survivors of bombed-out France, nursing the sick and helping to dig bodies from the ruins and, when the United Nations relief groups pulled out of Europe in 1952, she stayed on. In the wake of the war, and right up to the fall of the Iron Curtain, she personally drove heavy lorries from England to Poland loaded with donated medical and food supplies.

Deeply affected by all the horrors, deprivation and suffering that she had encountered Sue returned to Suffolk. She used her own savings to open the first home for 'forgotten friends of the allies' at her mother's old house, in the former village rectory at Cavendish, where she began caring for some thirty sick or injured survivors, mainly Poles. The Sue Ryder Foundation was born. By the following year the first nursing home was created in Suffolk and since then the name and reputation of the Foundation has become legendary. It provided, and continues to provide, homes and domiciliary care teams for the sick and disabled in any part of the world where there is a clear need and where the opportunity presents itself. Sue always intended that the Foundation should be a 'living memorial to the victims and opponents of tyranny and to those who suffer and die as a result of persecution'.

The course of her life was determined by two early influences, the example of her much-loved mother's voluntary social work, and by what she herself witnessed first in the depressed years of the 1930s and later during the war. In 1957 she married Group Captain Leonard Cheshire (1917–92), one of the country's best-known war heroes, who was already head of his own international charity, the Cheshire Foundation. In 1943, at the age of twenty-five, he became the youngest group captain in the RAF and was given command of 617 Squadron which developed new low-level marking techniques that dramatically increased bombing accuracy. He was awarded the Victoria Cross in 1944 after completing 100 bombing missions on heavily defended targets in Germany. Cheshire was the official British observer of the destruction caused by the nuclear bomb dropped on Nagasaki. Shocked at what he had seen, he dedicated the rest of his life to maintaining world peace.

When in 1979 Sue Ryder was offered a peerage she considered it for a long time and decided finally that a platform in the House of Lords would give her an opportunity to speak on issues close to her heart. She took the title Baroness Ryder of Warsaw, as a tribute to the Polish people, of whom she had grown so fond during her wartime resistance work, saying 'I feel I belong to Poland.' She spoke regularly in the House of Lords, especially in debates on the sick and disabled, unemployment and race relations. She worked indefatigably for her Foundation, often travelling up to 50,000 miles a year from her Suffolk home to attend official functions. When the Queen Mother opened the Sue Ryder Foundation Museum at Cavendish in 1979, Lady Ryder said it was a tribute not to herself but 'to all those who have suffered and who continue to suffer'.

Lord Cheshire died in 1992 and the last few years of Sue Ryder's life were clouded by ill health and a public row with her co-trustees over the management of the Foundation. In 1998 she retired as a trustee and set up a rival organisation, the Bouverie Foundation. She died in hospital at Bury St Edmunds in 2000.

The Sue Ryder Foundation continues the work that Sue Ryder started in 1953 and for over five decades its achievements have helped to transform the lives of hundreds of thousands of people. Today there are twenty care centres and 500 charity shops in the United Kingdom and its international services stretch from Macedonia to Malawi. Both the headquarters and the heart of the operation are still in Suffolk.

SIX

Suffolk sons

THERE ARE AS many definitions for sons of Suffolk as for daughters but few have such an exotic background as the Maharaja Duleep Singh, the last ruler of the Punjab, friend of Queen Victoria, and master at Elveden Hall at the southern edge of Thetford Forest. After Queen Victoria became Empress of India in 1876 she developed a deep and abiding interest in the culture and people of the subcontinent, which was reflected in the friendships she formed. At Osborne House, on the Isle of Wight, she entertained many Indians over the years, among them the fifteen-year-old Duleep Singh who visited the Queen and Prince Albert there in 1854. The Queen sketched him playing with her children and he was photographed by Prince Albert.

Duleep was born in Lahore in 1838, the son of a great Sikh warrior, the Maharaja Ranjit Singh. When in 1848 the British intercepted Ranjit Singh's attempt to invade and capture Afghanistan, he was tricked into signing a treaty that left his Punjabi borders undefined. Within a year the powerful 'Lion of the Punjab' was dead and his son Duleep inherited a vast fortune and, briefly, the legacy of ruler.

In 1849 the British annexed the Punjab and it was the end of the Sikh State. The eleven-year-old Maharaja Duleep Singh was deposed and all his properties and treasure, including the Koh-i-Noor diamond, were surrendered in return for a pension from the British government. Duleep was brought to England and in 1863 acquired the 17,000-acre Elveden Hall estate, just south of Brandon on the edge of Thetford Forest where he immediately embarked on an ambitious scheme of grandiose enhancement, described by Nikolaus Pevsner as 'an Oriental extravaganza unparalleled in England'. The Indian Hall is constructed from richly veined marble, with twenty-eight columns and three large galleries. The ornamented doors of the maharaja's 'pleasure dome' – a glass lantern, with walls, pillars and arches overlaid with Indian ornamental detail – are covered with beaten copper, and outside a majestic portico adorns the north aspect. For four years 150 men, many of them Italian craftsmen who carved the white Carrara marble *in situ*, worked at Elveden Hall to create what is little short of a maharaja's palace in the Suffolk countryside.

Here Duleep, with his wife and ten children, led the life of an English aristocrat. He entertained lavishly and gave huge hunting and shooting parties to which royalty and members of the aristocracy were invited. The maharaja himself was famously considered the fourth-best shot in England. In 1876 the Prince of Wales went to Elveden to enjoy Duleep Singh's hospitality and posed for a photograph that was sent to the queen at Osborne.

Duleep Singh's looks and manner particularly impressed the queen and the two became friends. Victoria was so taken with him that she commissioned the court artist Franz Winterhalter to paint his portrait and, later, porcelain images were made of the maharaja, his first wife Maharanee Bamba and their son Prince Victor Albert, named in honour of the royal couple. His second son, Prince Frederick, was educated at Eton and Cambridge University and went on to serve in the Suffolk Yeomanry.

Gradually, though, a deep rift began to develop between the Queen and Duleep Singh. He had converted to Christianity, but over the years began to regret not only the loss of his kingdom but also his religion, and he reconverted to Sikhism. He began to think that he had betrayed not only himself but also his people and when the British government would not address his grievances Duleep attempted to join forces with Irish Fenians and Russian revolutionaries, hoping to destabilise the British establishment. He also tried to recover the Koh-i-Noor diamond, which he said had been stolen from him, but it had already been given to the Queen, who took no small exception at being asked to return it.

Some years later, however, the Queen and the last maharaja of the Punjab were reconciled. They met while Victoria was holidaying in Nice, and to some extent were able to revive their friendship. Duleep Singh died in Paris in 1893, having been married to his second wife for just four years and his body was returned to Suffolk for burial.

Duleep Singh's legacy to Suffolk is the extraordinary mansion at Elveden and his memorial in the parish church which is a place of modern pilgrimage for Sikhs from across the world. All of the maharaja's ten children died childless and this is said to be the curse of the tenth guru, which visits the sins of the father, Ranjit Singh, on the son, Duleep. According to legend, the Sikhs' most important spiritual leader, Guru Gobind Singh, had a golden box of treasure buried at his death carrying with it the prophecy that anyone who touched it would 'vanish from the light'. But Ranjit Singh wanted to build a monument to the guru and dug up the box, so bringing the curse down on his family's head.

A curse of misfortune is also associated with the famed Koh-i-Noor diamond that was taken by the British from the maharaja and presented to Queen Victoria. It was later incorporated in the Queen Mother's crown to become part of the British crown jewels. The Queen Mother only ever wore the crown once, at the coronation of her husband, George VI, when she was crowned Queen Consort and Empress of India. In 2002 it rested on her coffin and was carried through London, in the funeral procession from St James's Palace to Westminster Hall. It was thought by some to be significant that she was the last crowned Empress of India. The diamond's curse was said to have come from the Hindu god Krishna from whom it was stolen as he lay sleeping. Another of the numerous Koh-i-Noor legends has it discovered in a riverbed in 3200 BC, but what is certain is that it was confiscated from the Suffolk maharaja in 1849 by British colonial officials who found it in the treasury of the Punjabi capital, Lahore. Its history had been synonymous with deceit, duplicity, brutality, torture, murder and mayhem and when Queen Victoria was made aware of this she immediately had it recut.

The quiet country churchyard of St Andrew and St Patrick at Elveden regularly sees pilgrimages to the grave of Duleep Singh, who lies beside his first wife with the ashes of his daughter Princess Catherine scattered nearby. Ajinder Chawla, President of the World Punjabi Organisation UK, recently led high-ranking Indian ministers to the graveyard and told the *East Anglian Daily Times*: 'We have always kept our memories in our hearts of Duleep Singh, who was the last Sikh ruler of the Punjab. He was buried here and we have a relationship with this particular place because he was the last ruler.'

The forces that brought the maharaja to Suffolk were in all respects different from those that brought another man here from closer to home. In 1985 a young jockey named Lanfranco Dettori came to England to serve his apprenticeship with the Newmarket-based trainer Luca Cumani. Lanfranco, better known as Frankie, was born in Sardinia in 1970, the son of Italian champion jockey Gianfranco Dettori and his wife, a circus performer who did back-flips standing astride two horses. When he was eight Frankie's father bought him a Palomino pony and when he was thirteen he sent him to a trainer in Pisa where he become a stableboy and apprentice jockey. At sixteen he came to Suffolk as an apprentice, earning just £12.50 a week.

Frankie Dettori was destined to become one of the best-known, and most easily identifiable, flat race jockeys since Lester Piggott and became the first teenager since Piggott to ride 100 winners in a single season. Even those with no knowledge of or interest in racing know the Dettori name, and his charismatic personality has taken him beyond racing into the world of entertainment. He has presented *Top of the Pops*, was the subject of *This is Your Life*, and has appeared on numerous quiz and interview shows on television. Currently he is team captain on the BBC television quiz *A Question of Sport*. As a concession to the female interest in Frankie Dettori there is a large poster of him semi-clothed in the ladies' cloakroom of the Racing Museum in Newmarket!

After his first winner in 1986 Frankie Dettori never looked back. His famous 'flying dismount' from the saddle after a big race win has become his trademark. He was champion jockey in 1994 and 1995, and in 1996 became a household name after riding all seven winners at an Ascot meeting. It is racing's gain that Frankie did not pursue his boyhood ambition of becoming a petrol-pump attendant!

In June 2000 Frankie's career almost came to a tragic end when he was involved in an air crash. The American-built twin-propeller Piper Seneca nose-dived into Devil's Dyke just after taking off from the airstrip alongside the July and Rowley Mile racecourse. Frankie and fellow jockey Ray Cochrane scrambled out of the luggage area at the back of the plane. Cochrane hauled the injured Frankie out of the plane but was beaten back by the heat as he went back to try and rescue the pilot. Speaking from Addenbrooke's Hospital in Cambridge, with his wife Catherine at his side, Frankie told how he and Cochrane had resigned themselves to death: 'The plane was out of control, going drastically right towards the dyke. The right engine was smoking. At this stage I was just very frightened, I thought it was the end.' Knowing that any minute the plane could explode Cochrane tried to fight the flames with his jacket in a desperate attempt to save the pilot. 'No words can describe the feeling of seeing somebody in a plane being burned and being helpless,' said Frankie afterwards.

It was several months before Frankie returned to the saddle but when he did it was clear that he had not lost his touch with either the horses or the public. The Newmarket crowd has taken him to their heart and as he nears the finishing post, the ground vibrating from the horses' hooves, the roar matches the thunderous chant of 'Frankie! Frankie!' and they look for the broad smile and ebullient jubilation as he punches the air, standing in the saddle to acknowledge the crowd – another winner, another athletic leap off his mount onto the Suffolk soil.

Frankie lives just outside Newmarket with his wife Catherine, a Cambridge graduate, and their three children and in 2001 was awarded an honorary MBE.

A Suffolk man who might well have identified with the courage and tenacity of Frankie Dettori was a local celebrity in his village of Boxford, a few miles east of Sudbury and west of Hadleigh. George 'Tornado' Smith was, by any standards, a man of eccentric habits. A writer in the *East Anglian Daily Times* said: 'If Suffolk wanted a 20th century-born and bred folk hero, the bespectacled motor-cycle rider from Boxford would seem to have most of the credentials. After all, there are not too many lion-walking, would-be round-the-world sailors who pay court fines with pennies and farthings, ride motor-cycles upside down and die rich bankrupts these days.'

Tornado Smith was indeed a man of many parts. Imagine the furore that would erupt today if a young man began taking his pet lion for walks on a chain round the lanes of Boxford, said lion being kept at the back of the pub. This is exactly what Tornado Smith did with his lioness, Briton, during the 1930s. The sight of Briton being taken for walks was a common sight until, that is, the complaints became too frequent to be ignored by the pub landlady, his mother.

Tornado was born in a cottage opposite the Saracen's Head, Newton Green, in 1908, and named George William Smith. His father, also named George, was a thatcher from Edwardstone and his mother, Liz, was from Boxford. Soon after Tornado was born the family moved to take on the Baker's Arms at Whitestreet Green, just south of Boxford, where three more sons were born – John, Stan and Basil. By 1921 Mrs Smith had taken over as landlady at the White Hart in Boxford, which she ran for thirty years.

When he was fourteen Tornado left school to take up an apprenticeship with a local wheelwright, Frank Self, but found it difficult to settle. He had plans to sail round the world and even began to build his own boat, though it was destroyed by fire. He had a succession of jobs before becoming an AA motorcycle patrolman; then he saw an advertisement for an assistant to work with a Wall of Death act in Newcastle. It appealed to him and he set off on the 500-odd mile round trip from Boxford to the Spanish City Amusement Park on his 350 cc AJS motorbike.

The Wall of Death is a huge barrel, around 18 feet high and 30 to 40 feet across, which became popular in America in the early 1900s and was part of the English fairground scene during the 1930s. Its wooden cylindrical chamber revolves at high speeds, the centrifugal force keeping the riders on the wall, around the top of which is a viewing platform where spectators stand. It came about following a ban on board tracks in America and during the 1940s became hugely popular, both there and in Europe, at any place of enter-tainment that could accommodate the barrels, which weigh close to twelve tons. Tornado Smith was one of the first English exponents of the art of riding the Wall of Death in England in the early 1930s and certainly the most famous.

For a brief period big cats were incorporated into the acts. There was 'Fearless Eggbert', a lion that chased the bikes up the Wall, and 'Pete', a lion trained by one of the famous Pelaquin family to ride on the bike's handlebars. Numerous lions and lionesses were trained to ride in converted sidecars. Tales of such adventure and excitement seized Smith's imagination; once he had ridden the Wall of Death himself he left the young Boxford apprentice wheelwright behind and became Tornado Smith, daredevil motorcycle rider.

After leaving Newcastle he got a job with a Wall group touring abroad. He performed all over Europe, but in Germany disaster struck. Someone played a joke on him by putting sugar into his petrol tank. His engine stopped and the resulting injuries were severe enough for him to leave the tour and return home to Boxford. But he was soon off again, this time joining Bertram Mills Circus, where he met a young woman on a cosmetics stall, Doris Craven. He said later in a magazine article: 'I swept her off her feet . . . I took her up on the handlebars and though she passed out with giddiness, and collapsed into my arms, on coming round she asked for more, so a Wall-rider she just had to be and, later, my wife.'

They married in 1934 and starred as a double act – Doris and Dare – and one of their stunts involved Doris being towed round behind Tornado's motorcycle on roller skates. Doris later changed her name to Marjorie and even encouraged her younger sister to take up wall-riding under the name 'Daredevil Kitty'.

When they were in Suffolk the couple lived behind the White Hart in a caravan, the 'Gipsy Moth', built by Tornado himself. He was a craftsman and amateur mechanic, as well as sketch artist and poet, but above all he loved his motorcycle. On one famous occasion in 1937 he was stopped for speeding on the Southend seafront. He turned up at the court on his penny-farthing bicycle with L-plates back and front, wearing a grey-check suit, green shirt, yellow pullover and red tie. According to Peter Haining in *Tornado Smith: Wall of Death Pioneer*, the accused made the following defence:

> I wish to plead for leniency on account of my nerves. I find that although I drive motor-cycles and motor cars on the Wall of Death at 60 mph, the signs and regulations on the road today make me nervous. I have 12 years driving experience but would, if you think it necessary, take the driving test. But at any rate in the meantime I must spend more time on my penny-farthing.

The judge was unmoved and fined him £7. Tornado paid £4 of it in ha'pennies and £1 in farthings. (In pre-decimal currency, there were 480 ha'pennies, and 960 farthings, to the pound!) While the court official counted out the farthings Tornado slipped one back into his pocket, so that the final count was a farthing short. Tornado demanded a recount, at which point the official ordered him off the premises. He went – complete with the farthing!

Tornado must have heard of, and perhaps even seen, motorcycle stunts involving lions and in the early 1930s bought a lioness cub from Chapman's Circus, and named her Briton. He trained her to ride on the handlebars and worked out a spectacular American-style act with Briton in a sidecar. Tornado, Doris and their lioness became a familiar sight around Boxford, with Briton sitting at the pub picnic table having tea with the couple, enjoying an ice cream, getting in and out of the family car and, of course, performing, first by sitting on a platform built over the handlebars of Tornado's high-powered Indian Scout motorcycle and then, when she grew too big for the platform, in a specially constructed side-car. Briton often gave the audience huge amusement when she refused to get off the platform at the end of the act, which she sometimes performed up to forty times a day. Photographs show a relaxed Tornado, wearing his familiar black beret with skull-and-crossbones badge and his tortoiseshell glasses, with his arm around Briton or playfully held in the lioness's mouth.

Every winter Tornado would bring Briton back to Boxford for the off-season and would entertain his mother's customers at the 'White Hart' by feeding the lioness pieces of meat direct from his mouth. In Tornado's scrapbook there were hundreds of photographs and articles about Briton who was for five years part of the Doris and Dare act. Then, when she was about five years old, she either broke a leg in her cage or, according to the more popular version, turned on her master and was shot. It emerged later that for Briton's lifetime Tornado had carried a small revolver with him, in case of emergency. Though the precise reason was never confirmed, it was always said that Tornado himself shot her with his revolver. Briton was buried on the pub forecourt and for many years the spot was marked by a small wooden headstone with the inscription:

BRITON
The Wall of Death She Rode with Safety,
In Her Cage She Met Her Doom.

For a time a little black lamb named Sparky was introduced into the act as a substitute for Briton. Sparky had similar tendencies to eccentricity that the late-lamented Briton had possessed and besides enjoying bathing in the sea at Southend with Doris, developed a taste for chewing tea leaves and cigarettes.

Tornado was often employed to repair and renovate a Wall of Death barrel, which was erected in the White Hart yard in the winter months. He performed locally and once took it on a mini-tour to Sudbury, where he enthralled a capacity audience with

daring deeds, the proceeds going to the British Legion. It was calculated that between 1929 and 1948 Tornado Smith travelled
110,000 miles inside the Wall of Death.

When war broke out in 1939, Tornado volunteered to be a
fighter pilot, but was rejected because of his poor eyesight. His
marriage to Doris was by this time on the rocks and when he joined
the Merchant Navy they divorced. After the war he remarried and
had a daughter, but that marriage failed and, after his second
divorce, he began touring again, this time in Spain. It was the last
his family heard of him until news arrived, in 1972, that he had
died in South Africa. Tornado Smith, the daredevil motorcycle rider
and fearless entertainer had died destitute, with debts amounting
to about £3,000.

At least that is what the family thought, until it was discovered
that in fact Tornado had owned over £200,000 in stocks and
shares. The story hit the headlines and it looked as though his
three brothers were in for an unexpected windfall from Tornado's
secret nest-egg. However, the publicity attracted the attention of
the Inland Revenue and the brothers were to see nothing of the
money. Three years after Tornado's death the tax authorities were
still mulling it over and eventually the state took it all.

A Suffolk man who had a different approach to eccentricity was
the cartoonist Carl Giles OBE (1916–95). A legend in his own lifetime – and a one-man national institution – the self-taught artist
and cartoonist more than caught the spirit of the age as for half a
century readers followed the exploits of the best-loved of all his
characters, the brolly-wielding Grandma and the pathetic Vera.
Every day for over fifty years he drew a topical cartoon for either
the *Daily Express* or *Sunday Express* and, in 1946, came the first Giles
annual for non-*Express* readers. He captivated the nation's heart
with his sympathetic comedy and identification with the common
man fighting an endless supply of life's little problems. His work is
a day-by-day social history of post-war Britain.

Like many Suffolk sons, Giles – as he is universally known –
was born in London, his father a shopkeeper and his grandfather
a jockey who rode for Edward VII. His first name was Ronald, but

as a young man he affected a hairstyle reminiscent of Boris Karloff, who had made his name playing Frankenstein's monster. Ronald's friends began to call him 'Karlo' – or Carlo – and so he became Carl Giles, later shortened to Giles. After leaving school at the age of fourteen, he began his career as a cartoon animator in London before landing a job working for Alexander Korda, a Hungarian who had emigrated to Hollywood during the 1920s but came to England in 1931. Korda is credited with saving the then struggling British film industry. After moving to *Reynold's News* as a cartoonist, Giles found a job in Ipswich and so began a love affair with Suffolk. In 1942 he married his first cousin, Joan Clarke, and the couple spent their honeymoon in the Dickens Suite of the Great White Horse in Ipswich. During the war, which saw Giles on active service, they rented Badger's Cottage, north of Ipswich, from an absent naval officer. When Joan was bombed out of her London home they moved to the tiny village of Tuddenham, a few miles from Woodbridge. During the latter part of the war Giles became fascinated by the American servicemen, shipped to Suffolk by the thousand from 1942 onwards, and his depiction of the cigar-chomping 'Yanks' was specially appreciated by the servicemen themselves. He and Joan became close friends with many GIs and formed a 'raggedy jazz band' – Giles on the piano – with two Americans he met in his local pub, The Fountain, at Tuddenham. They held open house for the men from the American bases and offered a special welcome to black GIs.

It was in 1943 that Giles's work was noticed by John Gordon, then editor of the *Sunday Express*, who offered him a job. After some persuasion he agreed and began a long association with the newspaper and its readership. He produced a staggering 7,500 cartoons depicting life as it was dealt to millions of families who identified with, and laughed at, the Giles Family.

Carl and Joan moved to their 280 acre farm at Witnesham, just outside Ipswich, where he lived for over fifty years. He worked from a studio in Ipswich from where he used to send his cartoons off to Fleet Street by train. He was notorious for being late with his copy, and editors used to send their men to wait anxiously on

Liverpool Street station for the next episode in the life of the Giles Family, the runner poised to rush it off to the office in time for the following morning's newspaper. In later years the rail service became erratic and unreliable so it went by taxi and in the late 1940s a helicopter was used during heavy snow.

At home in his seventeenth-century farmhouse, Giles and his wife would go through the day's newspapers and discuss subjects for the cartoon. In Suffolk he was able to draw on a particular type of Englishness and had the special advantage of seeing things from two viewpoints, the countryside and the town. After lunch Giles would leave for his Ipswich studio where, three hours later, the work would be finished and on its way to London by the afternoon train. Never political, his cartoons were intended to entertain yet were always meticulously researched, right down to the correct buttons on a Guardsman's uniform.

Ipswich station was not only essential for getting his work to London, but was also to play a large part in the social comings and goings of friends visiting Carl and Joan at their Suffolk farm. They had long and enduring friendships with Eric Sykes, Johnny Speight, Tommy Cooper and Michael Bentine, among others. Royal persons, too, were not immune to the Giles charm. He would regularly lunch with Prince Charles, and the Duke of Edinburgh was a confirmed collector of his work.

Just a short time before Giles died, in 1993, a statue was unveiled in Ipswich by the actor Warren Mitchell, Johnny Speight's 'Alf Garnett' in the television series *Till Death Us Do Part*. The bronze, by Ipswich sculptor Miles Robinson, includes Grandma, Rush the Dog, terrible twins Lawrence and Ralph and sickly Vera. It has no inscription beyond the famous 'Giles' signature and is sited at the junction of Princess Street and Queen Street, that part of Ipswich that Giles himself looked on daily from his office. Warren Mitchell said: 'A lot of cartoons are caricatures, but Giles' cartoons are of real people, I think he was a great artist. Most statues are ignored, but with this one, children will stop and say "What is that?" And their parents will have to explain.'

Giles died in 1995 and on top of his coffin, as it progressed down the aisle of Tuddenham church, was placed one of the terrible twins. He had been not only one of the nation's favourite cartoonists, but also an artist, musician, horseman, yachtsman, film maker, racing driver, draughts champion, farmer, engineer and craftsman. He loved Suffolk and lived happily at Tuddenham and Witnesham with his wife who, above all his other loves and passions, was the most important and significant factor in his life. In 1995 he was awarded the OBE and in 2000 he was posthumously voted 'Britain's favourite cartoonist of the twentieth century'. It should have come as no surprise to anyone who knew the depth, subtlety, significance and hefty dose of hidden agenda that characterises his work. It is worth seeking out the subversive activities that take place before your very eyes, and yet sometimes were missed for years, until a Giles annual was discovered, years later, on a family bookshelf or in a second-hand bookshop. In retrospect the topicality of the scene might well be lost, and certainly unfathomable to the generation that did not grow up with Giles. But it is a measure of his genius that it is invariably the undercurrents that give the work of Carl Giles that indefinable quality that is the cause of its endurance. Cartoonists come and go, but the magic of Giles transcends his generation.

A man who might well have inspired Giles in another era was a farmer from the nearby village of Playford, just south of Witnesham, half-way between Ipswich and Woodbridge. The name Herman Biddell is synonymous with agriculture, the establishment of the Suffolk Show and, most especially, the history of the Suffolk cart-horse, known affectionately as the 'Suffolk Punch'. In 1877 Biddell was asked to compile a Suffolk Horse Stud Book and then spent three years meticulously writing the first volume. It was a retrospective register of genuine Suffolk stallions and is a work of superlative excellence and accuracy. The heavy-horse historian Edward Hart wrote of Biddell: 'Of all the dedicated, enthusiastic, hard-working and unbiased breed society secretaries who have graced the British livestock industry, few have been the peer of Herman Biddell and none has excelled him. His industry and accuracy leap from the pages of that gigantic first stud book.'

Herman Biddell was born in Playford in 1832, the fourth son of

Arthur and Jane Biddell, and a big man in every respect: he stood 6 feet 4 inches tall and weighed 19 stone. Arthur Biddell, High Constable and Land Agent, had been a tenant farmer on 1,000 acres in Playford since the early 1800s, breeding Red Polled cattle a long time before other Suffolk breeders. Herman's interest was always the Suffolk Horse, the oldest pure heavy horse bred in Britain, which had been perfected by another son of Suffolk, Thomas Crisp, of Rendlesham and Gedgrave, in 1768. (The story goes that they were named Punches after an observation by the diarist and Master of the Guild of Trinity House, Samuel Pepys, on one of his many visits to Lowestoft to oversee the Guild's lighthouse. There he heard the parents of fat children with short legs address them as Punches. The Suffolk horse, too, was stocky, with relatively short legs, and so the name Punch was coined.)

Arthur's eldest son, George, became a civil engineer; his second son, William, became a Member of Parliament for West Suffolk. A frequent visitor to the Playford home was Arthur's nephew, Sir George Biddell Airy, 7th Astronomer Royal who, although self-educated, had an extensive private library and numbered among his friends many prominent figures in and around Ipswich. Sir George was Britain's first professional astronomer, in that he had no independent income and earned a living from his chosen career. He purchased a cottage in Playford to which he and his wife would retreat whenever he could from his busy life travelling all over the United Kingdom and Europe and the pressures of his work as Astronomer Royal. He retired to Suffolk in 1881 and was buried at Playford in the Airy-Biddell family tomb. He was renowned for his love of Suffolk and more than once said 'There is no county in England better than Suffolk.'

Brothers Manfred and Herman Biddell were both farmers and breeders of the Suffolk Horse, Herman following his father at Hill Farm, Playford. The Suffolk is always chesnut (traditionally spelt with no 't' after the 's') with seven shades of colour recognised: bright, red, golden, yellow, light, dark and dull dark. The legs are clean, with no 'feathers' (hair on lower legs), which make it an ideal animal for the heavy clay soils of Suffolk. In 1907 Herman

Biddell wrote: 'Those remarkable features, the uniformity of colour, the short leg, the rounded carcasses, the longevity with vitality, frequently reaching nearly 30 years of age, are still the well-known characteristics of the Suffolk Horse.' Some years later George Ewart Evans, a Welshman who made Suffolk his home and wrote *The Horse in the Furrow*, said:

> The Suffolk's great stamina and his particular shape or conforma-
> tion of deep, well-rounded body ('a good bread basket', as Suffolk
> horsemen said) enabled him to tackle the heavy clays and to work
> for a whole day's stint in the field without being fed, from the time
> of his 6 a.m. breakfast to his main meal between four and five in
> the afternoon.

Herman and Manfred began gathering material for a history of the Suffolk Punch in 1862, realising that the facts, histories and pedigrees were fast receding into the 'land of oblivion' and existed only in the memories of elderly men. Herman wrote an account of the various sources for the stud book:

> I was introduced to the name of old John Moyse. To those who
> knew that extraordinary man, the value of the introduction will be
> readily understood. Born in 1789 at the Queen's Head, at
> Stradbroke, and apprenticed to a barber at Halesworth, he comm-
> enced business at Earl Soham. Here he took to colt-breaking, shifted
> his tent to Occold, near Eye, became a dealer in horses and moved
> to Framlingham. There he failed in the horse business, and once
> more set up his pole, and after resting on his oars for a time
> became a recipient of one of the town charities, and eventually
> ended his days in Sir Robert Hitcham's Alms House.

John Moyse lived to be ninety and had made a study of the Suffolk Horse all his life. He was, wrote Biddell, a 'walking stud book'. Another man of ninety who had worked with horses all his life was also on Biddell's list, but the man unfortunately lost his mind before he could be interviewed. By the time Biddell met him he could barely remember his own name.

For fifteen years Biddell collected and recorded the information until at a meeting of the Suffolk Agricultural Association at Ipswich in 1877 it was proposed that a Suffolk Stud-book Association be formed. The patron was the Earl of Stradbroke, of Henham Hall, and Arthur Crisp, grandson of the original Punch breeder, shared the administration with Herman, while Manfred was treasurer. They were shortly to prove that all true Suffolks were descended from a single horse bred by Thomas Crisp in 1768. During the three years it took to compile the stud book and history of the breed Biddell traced 1,236 stallions spanning 120 years. He gave up all his other interests, including drawing, politics and even farming, to concentrate on the register.

The entries in over 700 pages of the first volume of the History read like poetry and are a masterpiece of contemporary English, brimming with humour and anecdotes, written by a man who had no education beyond the village school. Many of the entries contain details of who had sold a horse to whom, in what parish, and for how much money. Descriptions of every stallion he could trace, alive or dead, were listed together with their offspring wherever they were known or could be discovered, good or bad. Of 'Duke', bred by Mr D. Barker of Bruisyard, he wrote: 'A savage brute – not much used as a sire: sold by Mr. Grout, kicked out the end of his box on the railway, and was shipped for the continent to diffuse the cranky temper of his maternal grandsire among the German mares.' Of 'Captain', bred by Mr C. French of Ramsholt, he wrote: 'Dark in colour, a thick heavy horse with a bad temper. He travelled several years, and was then bought by Mr Wilson, of Baylham Hall, who resold him to Mr Blotfield, of Helmingham. He was a quick tempered animal to manage: his dam, an inveterate kicker, ran away with a waggon and killed a man.'

Published in 1880, Biddell's first volume is illustrated by the Ipswich artist John Duvall (1816–92), who was commissioned to paint oil portraits of the horses, though eventually only his sketches were used. Biddell had great admiration for Duvall: 'It is easy enough to give an outline; and with a bald face, three white legs, and some unmistakable colour, to call the picture a portrait. But Mr Duvall has had to deal with very different material. To produce individuality of character in the portrait of a Suffolk horse, required no little practice.'

Although Biddell also wrote *Agriculture of Suffolk*, for the Victoria History of the Counties of England series, he is best remembered for *The Suffolk Stud Book*. He also contributed to *The Horses of the British Empire* and sundry political pamphlets. In addition he played cricket in county and local clubs, was an alderman of the East Suffolk County Council for fifteen years and farmed several hundred acres. His brother Manfred also farmed at Playford, and his brother William at Lavenham Hall.

Herman Biddell died in 1917. He had been sole churchwarden of the parish of Playford for forty-four years but when the vicar pointed out to him that the law required two, Biddell regarded the idea as preposterous and resigned. It was, he told the vicar, a waste of time for two men to do what one could manage equally well.

A Suffolk man who can also be thought of as having done the work of two is Lewis Ernest Watts Mills, better known as the internationally famous actor of stage and screen, John Mills. He not only began his career in Suffolk but his name (which he changed from Lewis to John when he was ten) was immortalised in the county when, in 1988, a small theatre in Ipswich was named after him.

Born in 1908, John Mills's early life was spent at Belton, just north of Lowestoft (then in Suffolk but lately removed to Norfolk), where his father was headmaster at the local school. He looked back on that time 'with little or no affection', part of the problem being that he was the headmaster's son. However, fishing trips to nearby Gorleston and an 'army' of friendly aunts helped, as did visits from his older sister, Annette (later to find television fame with 'Muffin the Mule'). Being a dancer she taught him what became his 'speciality' – the sailor's hornpipe – reinforcing his early desire to become an entertainer. By chance, when he was sent to St John Leman's School in Beccles, the headmaster happened to be a keen theatre-goer. John landed the part of Puck in *A Midsummer Night's Dream* and gave his first public performance.

When he left school the family moved to Felixstowe from where John applied for his first job, in the offices of R & W Paul, situated on Ipswich docks. It was to be memorable only for the small part he played in the 1926 General Strike. He had only just moved from the inside office to the shipping department and remembers his time there as both 'deadly' and 'monotonous', enlivened only by the exciting few days of the strike when white-collar workers were required to help keep the goods moving. In his autobiography *Up in the Clouds, Gentlemen Please* he wrote: 'A notice appeared on the board stating that the police needed volunteers to act as special constables, and one of our directors had added a rider to the effect that any of the staff who felt it their duty to answer the call to arms would be granted indefinite leave from the office on full pay.' One of their first assignments was to supervise grain being unloaded from one of the barges and they were instructed to line up to prevent strikers from disrupting the work. They were also warned to look out for the women, who would bring sandwiches and flasks for the strikers.

Lined up in front of the strikers the office workers stared at them in horror, knowing they were no match for them if a fracas broke out. After two hours neither side had made a move other than to glare at one another across the dock. Then the wives arrived and broke the deadlock. One large female began a one-woman attack on the office workers and advanced on the diminutive John Mills 'like a large, black barge in full sail' firing derogatory remarks in his direction. Shortly afterwards, however, they and the strikers dispersed for lunch and Mills and his colleagues were glad to retreat to the safety of the office where they were relieved of their armbands and wooden truncheons.

While living in Felixstowe he joined two amateur dramatic societies, both of which had high standards and were able to put on shows at the Felixstowe Playhouse and fill it for a week. But before long he began to hanker after the bright lights of London and went to stay with his sister Annette, who had a job as an exhibition dancer. In 1929 he began his stage career as a £4-a-week chorus boy at the London Hippodrome before joining a troupe called The Quaints. He set off on a theatrical tour of the Far East, where he met his future wife Mary Hayley Bell (who went on to write *Whistle Down the Wind*).

In 1933 he made his first film, *The Midshipmaid*, followed by three others in the same year. Five years later he came to international prominence for his role in *Goodbye, Mr Chips* and soon afterwards began a string of patriotic roles that were to make him one of the best-known British actors of his era. *In Which We Serve* was followed by *We Dive at Dawn*, *Above Us The Waves*, *Scott of The Antarctic* and *Tunes of Glory*. In a career spanning over seventy years, John Mills has starred in more than a hundred films and above fifty theatrical performances. His brilliant portrayal of a deformed mute in *Ryan's Daughter* brought him a Hollywood Oscar in 1971. 'I'm not one of those who decry Oscars,' he said. 'Ever since school I've always liked the idea of competition and prizes.'

Mills was knighted for his services to the film industry in 1976 and numerous awards have come his way during a career that has spanned seven decades. In 1987 he appeared in Madonna's film *Who's That Girl?* and in 2002, at the age of ninety-four, he was honoured with a British Academy Fellowship at a Bafta tribute.

In 1988 the newly formed Eastern Angles, founded by actor and playwright Ivan Cutting, took over an old Drama Centre studio in Ipswich, which he wanted to rename. Ivan said:

> There was something in the local paper about Sir John Mills celebrating his eightieth birthday and the fact of his having worked on the docks here in Ipswich, just as we got news of taking over the old Drama Centre. We decided it needed a new name and we'd just done a play about life during the last war on the home front and Sir John seemed like a good person to name our new theatre after.

Sir John agreed to be their patron and the Drama Centre was renamed the Sir John Mills Theatre. In 2000 the Suffolk College in Ipswich recommended him for a University of East Anglia honorary degree of Doctor of Letters and he attended the degree ceremony in October of that year. He also took the opportunity to visit the theatre. He told the *East Anglian Daily Times*: 'I loved living in Felixstowe and have very happy memories of being near the sea and that's where I started acting.'

SEVEN

Clubbed to death: the murder of Suffolk's richest woman

SINCE THE NEWLY restored King Charles II made Newmarket famous in 1660, the West Suffolk town and its attendant racecourses have attracted royalty, the rich and famous, and no small number of eccentrics. Dukes, earls and the wealthy horse-owning elite invariably owned or rented houses in Newmarket, frequenting it only during race meetings, but nevertheless maintaining year-round stabling for the horses and a retinue of domestic staff. Charles II's most famous mistress, Nell Gwynne, had a house there and spent much of her time in it. In the 1940s and 1950s, however, several racehorse owners eschewed London and moved wholesale to Newmarket. One of the more famous was the heiress Dorothy Paget who financed her horse-racing from a vast inherited fortune.

It was said that Dorothy Paget made up for the plainness of her appearance by having what many thought was rather too much character. She changed her trainers with alarming regularity, though many might have been glad to find other employment since they had to put up with endless night-time telephone calls. Dorothy dined at seven o'clock, morning not evening, and slept for the rest of the day. She breakfasted at 8.30 in the evening, followed by numerous meals throughout the night. She disliked humans, especially men, who were said to make her vomit. When she kissed her horse Golden Miller after one of his many victories on the racecourse, an observer speculated that this was probably the first time she had kissed a member of the opposite sex – and a gelding, at that!

Other, more romantic women are associated with Newmarket, including Lily Langtry (later Lady de Bathe), one of a long line of royal mistresses of Edward VII, who during race meetings took rooms in the town with the actress. Lily owned a training stable and played an influential role in Edward's racing activities. Edward VII did not, though, follow his ancestor, Charles II, who was so enamoured of racing that he moved the court to Newmarket in the spring and autumn of each year and rode in races himself, the Rowley Mile course being named after his hack. He watched the horses from a shelter at the top of Warren Hill, now known as Kings Chair, often with his mistresses.

But of the several women of fortune who came to Newmarket few were as rich, or eccentric, as the heiress and socialite Rachel Parsons, who in 1946 bought Branches Park, in Cowlinge. Ten years later the woman who had everything – money, education and a potentially brilliant career as an engineer – had become a curmudgeonly, belligerent and foul-mouthed bully who was clubbed to death by a stableman over the matter of a few pounds.

It had all started so promisingly. Rachel Parsons was the daughter of the Honourable (later Sir) Charles Algernon Parsons (1854–1931), fourth son of the 3rd Earl of Rosse, and one of the greatest engineers of the twentieth century. His father had represented Dublin University and County Longford in the Irish Parliament and was renowned in scientific annals for astronomical discoveries. His reflecting telescope weighed three tons and contained a mirror that was six feet in diameter, while the tube was fifty-six feet in length.

In the 1870s his son Charles was one of those industrialists faced with the challenge of providing the country with the increasingly large amounts of power demanded by burgeoning British industry. Steam engines were too large and noisy and Parsons realised the need for a rotating machine, or turbine, which would convert the power of steam directly into electricity. He set about building his first multi-stage reaction turbine in 1884 and became a junior partner in the firm Clarke, Chapman and Parsons. It is said that Parsons sketched the original design for the reaction blades on the back of an envelope. After two years, and a £100,000 research investment, he set up the Parsons Marine Steam Turbine Company and wrote himself into world industrial history. In 1899 a turbine drive destroyer, HMS *Viper*, capable of thirty knots, was launched and by the time of the Battle of Jutland in 1916, his turbines were powering super dreadnoughts.

In 1883 Charles Parsons married Katherine Bethell and they had two children, a son and a daughter. Rachel Mary Parsons was born in 1885 and adopted the family mantle of scientist and engineer at her father's knee. Charles Parsons took out over 300 patents and many of these inventions, including a powered model helicopter, monoplane and three-wheeled go-cart, came about as a means of entertaining his children. Rachel was nothing less than a child prodigy. She was educated at Roedean and became the first woman to take the Engineering Tripos at Newnham, which she gained with honours. She became an associate Member of the Institution of Naval Architects and in 1918 the only woman to hold a master mariner's ticket.

The first cloud on an otherwise happy and fulfilled horizon came in 1918 when her adored brother, and heir apparent to the internationally renowned firm of Parsons, was killed in the trenches. During the war Rachel had taken his place in the family business and proved herself an able substitute. She organised the employment of women in her father's engineering works, then in the training department of the Ministry of Supply. With her mother she sat on the National Council of Women and in 1919 mother and daughter were co-founder members of the Women's Engineering Society. She met and fell in love with a young man . . . and another cloud appeared. Her parents considered him 'unsuitable' and she was made to give him up. He later went on to become an internationally famous diplomat. Those who knew her well said that she never got over it.

Her life was further blighted when the war ended and her father, old-fashioned even by 1920s standards, thought it unseemly that a woman should be seen to work actively in commercial industry during peacetime. She was forced to apply her highly trained and brilliant mind to domestic matters: a career in anything but home making and providing future wife material for an approved man, was barred to her.

Her years at university wasted, and the practical knowledge built up during the war years dismissed as irrelevant, she began rebelliously to organise lavish and ostentatious parties for the cream of society first at her house in Grosvenor Square and then in Belgrave Square. To try to occupy her mind Rachel became a member of the London County Council and an understandably ardent supporter of women's rights.

In 1931 her father died and she inherited over £1 million. Rachel Parsons was at last free to see whoever she pleased and, with the backing of high-powered contacts, her money gave her the opportunity to do pretty well whatever she chose. But by then she was out of the habit of engineering and firmly in the habit of partying. In 1939 she hosted one of the last great parties before the Second World War, attended by members of the royal family and London's high society.

In 1946 she left London and moved to Newmarket in Suffolk. Perhaps as a result of her Irish ancestry, Rachel Parsons had an enduring passion for horse-racing and, since everything else that she had most wanted had been denied her, she used part of her inheritance to buy Branches Park. This 2,600-acre estate lay in Cowlinge not far from Newmarket and half-way between Bury St Edmunds and

Haverhill. The estate had an eighteenth-century mansion with ten reception rooms, thirty-seven bedrooms and a swimming pool. To finance the purchase of a second house on the racecourse side of Newmarket, she sold a 10,000-acre property in Northumberland. The second property was Lansdowne House, which had extensive stables where Rachel planned to train her yearlings.

At first Rachel Parsons had beginner's luck. But her wealth allowed her to indulge both herself and her horses, and this was ultimately to prove disastrous. The horses were overfed, not by her trainers or grooms, but by Rachel herself who often slipped out to the stables at night with titbits. The famous Le Dieu d'Or, which had run a successful season for her as a two-year-old and was a difficult horse by any standards, began to deteriorate as it became seriously overweight.

Those who met Rachel were struck first by her extraordinary appearance. Short and stout, she wore an auburn wig, strands of which hung down over her shoulders under a huge Edwardian hat. Her clothes were ill-matched and tatty; her canvas shoes dirty; and she invariably wore one of her several long, and very expensive, fur coats. She regularly wore a mink coat to mix animal feed. Her beautiful voice, always considered one of her best assets, contrasted with her untidy, unkempt appearance. In due course, though, the voice became coarse and she rarely spoke, only shouted. Her dresses quickly became dated, as she ceased to buy new ones, and the long flowing skirts of Edwardian England and the plumed hats that she always wore became her trademark. Often her stockings appeared to be falling down and she would commonly wear a nylon on one leg, the other encased in a woollen sock with a hole in it.

Only when she went to a race meeting did she make any attempt to dress normally. Then, she would go in an open-top Rolls Royce and sit in the back seat, eating sardines out of the tin. (In fact she kept eight cars but was often seen thumbing a roadside lift from a passing lorry.)

Rachel's outward appearance mirrored what was happening at Branches Park. She lived in only two rooms, which over time degenerated from being filthy to becoming a positive health hazard. She shared this den with an Airedale called Bruce and twenty cats. A Jersey cow was kept purely to provide Bruce and the cats with milk and twice a week she took a taxi to buy dog biscuits and a large number of eggs, which she mixed together in saucepans that were never cleaned and became encrusted with the uneaten remains.

The sumptuous indoor swimming pool was used to store hay while oats were stored in the squash court. Vegetables, horse feed and sundry objects in varying stages of decay adorned the state banqueting hall and everywhere there were empty sardine cans, bottles and eggshells. Water began to seep in through the roof. Wherever there was rotting or uncovered food the place was overrun with rats and mice, and this included the training establishments. All but a few of the mansion's sixty-eight rooms were locked and unused, chiefly for fear of theft by staff and of outside intruders, a fear that turned into an obsession.

In spite of her wealth Rachel Parsons became mean, so mean that she begrudged paying her staff wages. She argued with the tradesman over every last ha'penny and became convinced that her staff were stealing from her. Eventually, all the doors in the mansion were locked. Her proclaimed love of animals did not extend to human beings and she became increasingly withdrawn. Her domineering ways, and foul, abusive language, meant that no one would work for her for long whilst her method of paying her employees became eccentric: she carried hundreds of pounds in notes in her handbag and paid the men in cash. Invariably they had to ask for their wages, when she would quarrel with them. She had been known to drive across ploughed fields in a Daimler to sack a member of staff.

In March 1956 what Rachel Parsons had feared for years actually happened when burglars broke into the house. She decided she would leave the mansion and go to live at Lansdowne House. Her regular taxi driver could pick her up daily so that she could visit her precious, and much-loved horses, plus the cats and the unfortunate Bruce, who had been left behind in the rat-infested room, formerly shared with his mistress.

Rachel was now sixty-eight years old. She still had a great deal of money but refused to pay her staff even the smallest amount of wages without a fight. She had no friends, was loathed by everyone with whom she had contact, and had long since exhausted the goodwill of the racing fraternity and the Jockey Club (with whom she argued constantly). Branches Park was reduced to a shocking state of disrepair and dilapidation and Lansdowne House and its attendant stabling was going the same way.

On Sunday, 1 July 1956 Rachel answered her door to find one of her former employees, Dennis Pratt, on the doorstep. A former apprentice jockey, Pratt had been employed to look after the horses, in particular Le Dieu d'Or, but was then out of work having left the Parsons employ with two weeks' holiday money owing. He was twenty-six, married with two children and his wife was expecting a third. He had very little to lose by trying to get his money. He had attempted to see her twice before, but she had called the police. Dennis Pratt, however, was desperate.

Rachel opened the door in her usual aggressive and abusive manner, telling Pratt she was not going to pay him anything. But this time he was not going to be put off. He was fed up with her mean and petty attitude to what was, after all, a very small amount of money to her but all the world to him and his family. What happened next did not become apparent for another couple of days.

A jeweller in Cambridge contacted the police to say that a man calling himself Alan Poulson was trying to sell him a pair of binoculars. He said they had belonged to his dead father but the jeweller thought there was something strange about 'Mr Poulson' and that they might be stolen. The police interviewed 'Alan Poulson' and after finding two cameras and two travelling clocks in his briefcase asked him to go with them to the police station, which he did. There he was asked to turn out his pockets, which again he did without argument or protest, and laid out a total of £23 in cash. Where, enquired the police, had the money, the cameras and clocks come from? Obviously they were stolen, but where from?

Then, without provocation, Dennis Pratt broke down. They were from Lansdowne House in Newmarket, he admitted, and he had taken them from his old employer Rachel Parsons. He began sobbing and told the police his real name, the story about the holiday money, and the ensuing argument. At this stage the police still thought that they had in custody nothing more than a petty thief. Then he told them the rest of the story. Rachel had not just argued with him but had begun hitting him with her handbag and shouting at him. He lost his temper and picked up an iron bar from the ground beside the yard door. Still Rachel Parsons shouted at him and tried to hit him again . . . then he struck out. He hit her on the head with the iron bar and had, he presumed, killed her.

The police were astonished and immediately sent officers to Lansdowne House but found nothing. The place was a mess but they could find no body.

Pratt then told police that he had dragged her body into the pantry. In his statement he said:

> I picked her up by the shoulders and she was breathing heavily. She was really heavy. I did not know what to do. I stood with her and held her head. I did not know whether to run away or not. It was just getting dark and I could not help her. I must have realised it was too late to help her. I tried to sit her up. She gave a heavy gasp like a gurgle and stopped breathing.

On a second visit the police found the body: Rachel Parsons was indeed dead, 'clubbed to death' as the *Daily Telegraph* put it in a headline the next day.

After realising that she was dead, Pratt had not been entirely sure what to do, but he found Rachel's handbag and took from it what he thought she owed him. He found some keys and went up to one of the bedrooms, where he took the binoculars, cameras and clocks, together with some beads. Then he dragged the body to the pantry and left the house, locking the front door as he went. On arriving home he checked on his wife, who was in bed asleep, and made himself a cup of tea. Some time later he cycled back to Lansdowne House. His statement continued: 'I went back to where I had put her, in the pantry. She was lying in the same position. I felt her throat and she was dead, cold. I closed the pantry door.'

He then locked the house up again, threw the iron bar into the coke shed, and went to buy chocolate for the children. Later, without even changing his blood-soaked trousers, he tried to sell the binoculars.

Dennis Pratt was committed for trial at Newmarket magistrate's court on 24 July 1956, although he had done the prosecution's job for them. Indeed, had he not confessed it would have taken the police some time to identify him as a possible suspect, given that there were so many others. If he had wiped his fingerprints off the iron bar, destroyed or at least washed his trousers and laid low without trying to sell the stolen items, Dennis Pratt might well have got away with it.

It would also have been some time before anyone realised that anything was wrong at Lansdowne House. Pratt had left the bedroom lights on when he left the first time (Rachel always slept with the lights on) and turned them off when he returned, opening the curtains. Besides which, Rachel led such an eccentric lifestyle that there was no 'normal' behaviour as such.

Rachel's funeral was at St Mary's Church in Newmarket on 6 July. About fifty people attended, most of them women who were, reported the press, on their way to the main shopping centre a short distance away and stood in the church grounds as the cortège arrived. Fearing a demonstration by supporters of Pratt, the police provided a guard both for the service and the interment at Newmarket cemetery, which was closed for two hours before the burial.

Dennis James Pratt was committed for trial for murder and appeared before Chelmsford Assizes in November 1956. The judge was Mr Justice Diplock. Pratt was defended by Michael Havers (later Attorney General and, as Lord Havers, Lord High Chancellor), who told the court that his client denied murder: he would ask the jury to return a verdict of manslaughter on the grounds of provocation. Witnesses for the defence all told the same story of Rachel's lifestyle and how badly she treated employees. One of her former trainers told how he lost three stones in weight while working for her and how she abused him verbally. The defence was anxious to establish what kind of woman it was who had driven Pratt to do what he did. One witness described the deceased as 'an eccentric, quarrelsome, unpleasant old woman, dirty in her habits and uncontrolled in her language'.

Mr Havers told the court that the defendant, whom he described as 'of below-average intelligence', had no previous convictions, and read out extracts from a doctor's report to the effect that Pratt had acted under the influence of powerful emotions, which had blinded him to what he was doing. If there had been no iron bar to hand he might well not have killed her. They might have argued and no doubt she would have called the police, but he had not gone there to do her harm. Only to get what he thought he was owed in the way of holiday pay.

When the defendant took the stand he described how he and his wife had been abused, and what happened on the night of 1 July. He was still virtually in shock, and told the court, 'I do not remember how many times I struck her. I can hardly realise I have done it now.' He told how she had attacked him with her handbag and how he had tried to protect himself. It was, he said, all like a dream.

Unfortunately for Dennis Pratt it had not been a dream. The jury decided that he had not premeditated her death but that he had caused it. They brought in a verdict of manslaughter and Mr Justice Diplock sentenced him to ten years.

Inevitably Rachel's death was reported in all the local and national newspapers. She was, if nothing else, a superb vehicle for press sensationalism. The reporters revelled in her peculiarities and eccentricities. Her distinguished past, her former potential brilliance at engineering and acute business acumen were noted and contrasted with the sad figure presented by the Rachel Parsons of 1956. Shortly after her death the much-loved, but equally sad, Bruce was released from his room at Branches and her fifty-three racehorses sold for a total of £53,145 – a fortune in those days.

Rachel Parsons died intestate but, in addition to the sale of the racehorses, she left just over £600,000 plus Branches and Lansdowne House, all of which was shared between thirty relatives. Branches Park was put on the market but it was in a poor state and failed to reach its reserve price. Rainwater was pouring in through the roof and almost ten years of neglect had taken its toll. The estate was eventually sold privately and the mansion, built in 1739, demolished.

It is hard to lay blame for what happened to Rachel Parsons. Certainly Dennis Pratt was as much a victim as perpetrator of evil intent and there is no doubt that she had driven many others to the same point he had reached on that fateful night.

Might the real culprit have been Sir Charles Parsons, whose Victorian attitudes forbade her marriage to the man she loved and then deprived her of the use of a brain which he himself had been instrumental in developing? Yet Charles Parsons was a man of his time and what he did, he did with the best of intentions and with the blessing of contemporary society. Many women in Rachel's position found ways out of their social straightjackets without ruining their lives, but she did not – perhaps because of the broken love affair.

When Dennis Pratt was sentenced he broke down in court and tears streamed down his face. His third child had by then been born and while he was incarcerated in prison his wife would have to cope with three small children on her own. Chance had played a miserable part in his life and in the life, and eventual death, of Rachel Parsons.

EIGHT

Who killed Rose Harsent?

DURING THE NIGHT of Saturday, 31 May 1902, a terrible storm raged over Suffolk, the worst in living memory. For almost an hour lightning struck again and again and thunder shook the earth. Children and animals cowered in fright as torrential rain fell mercilessly on the village of Peasenhall, lying midway between Framlingham and Halesworth. At Providence House the Crisps came downstairs to check that the water had not risen far enough to enter the house. Later, Mrs Crisp said she heard a thud, followed by a scream, but the storm made it difficult to hear properly; her husband, a retired tailor, was deaf and heard nothing.

By Sunday morning the rising water had overflowed the brook which ran through the village centre and flooded out over the road and low ground on the eastern side towards Sibton. With difficulty William Harsent made his way to Providence House, where his twenty-three-year-old daughter Rose was employed as a maid, but he did not turn back. Even though it was only the other side of the village he visited her every Sunday bringing her clean linen from home. Storm or not, this Sunday would be no different.

But it was different. It was a day that would haunt William Harsent for the rest of his life and a day that is still talked about a hundred years later. What happened then has featured in numerous books and been cited in textbooks of criminology. He found his daughter lying dead in a pool of blood near the stairs which led to her attic room, with her throat cut and stab wounds to her neck and shoulder. There were cut marks to her hands where she had tried to shield herself from her attacker, and one arm was outstretched towards the scullery wall while her head rested against the steps leading to her attic bedroom. Her nightgown was burnt, leaving her almost naked, with broken glass from a lamp, spilt paraffin and semi-burned newspaper and ashes strewn around her charred body.

The coroner attended at the Swan Inn in Peasenhall and evidence was taken. At first the doctor said that Rose had taken her own life. Unmarried and six months pregnant, she had as much reason as any to despair of her predicament, though she had denied her condition to both her parents and her employers.

The suicide theory was soon overturned. Rose would hardly have stabbed herself, slit her own throat, disposed of the knife and then tried to set her own body on fire. Bruising was discovered on her right cheek and the post mortem evidence of her pregnancy convinced police that this was not suicide. Rose, and her unborn child, had been murdered in her employer's kitchen at Providence House on the night of 31 May 1902.

When news of Rose's death became public the village was shocked. Nothing like it had occurred in this sleepy village, deep in rural Suffolk, where life went on at an even and laborious pace. Almost immediately the finger was pointed at William Gardiner, a local man who worked at the Smyth Drill Works in Peasenhall, and whose relationship with Rose had given rise to gossip. Gardiner was a leading figure at the local Methodist church and he was also married. His wife Georgianna had consistently refused to believe the scandal put about the parish concerning her husband and Rose. Almost all the men of the village worked at Smyth's and it was a very close-knit, if not always harmonious, village. Any whiff of a scandal was sniffed out and fought over by the 700 or so inhabitants of Peasenhall and its twin village of Sibton, especially if it involved adultery and a man of the church.

For over a year there had been allegations, and even an inquiry by the Methodist Superintendent, about Gardiner's relationship with Rose, but it was eventually abandoned due to lack of hard evidence or a confession from either party. Gardiner told his wife he would end the association to stop the gossip. As foreman at the Drill Works, he was a man whose authority was enhanced by his role as Sunday School superintendent at the Sibton Primitive Methodist chapel. Although he had started life as the son of an unmarried woman, who had given birth in the Bulcamp Workhouse, Gardiner had done well for himself and was seemingly above reproach. He was also an assistant steward and choirmaster, which latter occupation brought him into contact with the young women of the village, including Rose who was in the choir. The *East Anglian Daily Times* later gave its readers a description of Gardiner: 'He is a man of striking and rather intelligent appearance. His forehead is very broad and moderately high: his eyes are black and piercing: nose large and slightly aquiline: the hair and complexion so intensely dark as to suggest the Spaniard rather than the Englishman.'

Georgianna fought hard to keep her husband's name out of the mud but it became difficult when two young men – George Wright and Alphonso Skinner – told tales of seeing Rose going into the old thatched building known as the Doctor's Chapel, just across the street from Providence House. Built originally in the late seventeenth century, the chapel was on land owned by Dr Lay. It was, until 1912, a Congregationalist Chapel where the Crisps worshipped and it was part of Rose's duties, as their maid, to clean it. Wright and Skinner, however, said she had gone there to meet Gardiner. They claimed to have crept up to the chapel and eavesdropped on 'naughty conversation' and 'shameless activity' that was going on inside. They said they heard two voices giggling and laughing, and the rustling of clothing and a woman's voice crying out – 'Oh, oh!'

Frightened that she would be dismissed from Providence House, Rose had denied any wrongdoing. Mrs Crisp had taken her on in 1900 but almost immediately gossip started over her interest in the young men of the village. A young man named Frederick Davis, who worked in the grocery store across the street from Providence House, used to send her salacious and racy love letters and she learned to recite the lewd poems and verses that other young men taught her. One wanted to marry her, but it was her association with Gardiner that attracted the most attention.

On the morning of 1 June 1902, a short time after William Harsent made his terrifying discovery, authority appeared in the shape of the village constable, PC Eli Nunn. Dr Lay came next and it was he who first suggested suicide (although the throat had been cut from left to right, severing the windpipe and left jugular vein, and a mixture of blood and paraffin was found on the lamp used to ignite the night-dress, apparently after death). Close behind came reporters from the *East Anglian Daily Times* which was to record events meticulously for the next two years, sometimes taking up two or three pages in the daily newspaper. (When the trial began, most of the court dialogue was repeated verbatim and long paragraphs were devoted to recording every move made in the courtroom.)

By the Tuesday it was clear to the police that there was only one man in the frame and late on Tuesday evening PC Nunn went with a warrant to arrest William Gardiner for the murder of Rose Harsent. An unsigned letter, posted on 31 May in Yoxford, had been found in Rose's bedroom that said: 'I will try to see you tonight at 12 o'clock at your place if you put a light in your window at 10 o'clock for about 10 minutes then you can take it out again and don't have a light in your room at 12 as I will come round to the back.'

Although it was unsigned it was presumed to have been written by Gardiner, which together with other incriminating evidence found at the scene, and the scandal surrounding his relationship with Rose, left the police in no doubt that there was enough evidence for an arrest. He was taken from his home at Alma Cottage to Saxmundham police court where magistrates committed him into custody for trial at the next Suffolk Assizes, due to begin in

November at Shire Hall, Ipswich. Gardiner, however, denied the crime at his arrest and steadfastly thereafter.

The trial opened on 5 November 1902 before Mr Justice William Grantham at the Suffolk Autumn Assizes in Ipswich. The case for the Crown was led by no less a figure than Henry (later Sir Henry) Fielding Dickens KC. Henry was the son of the famous novelist, Charles Dickens, and his fame added to public interest in the trial. The county's newspaper-reading public was reminded that it was at the Great White Horse Hotel in Ipswich that the famous incident in *The Pickwick Papers* took place, when Pickwick wandered into the wrong room and surprised a lady in bed with her curlers in! The Suffolk village of Blundeston gave Dickens the name for David Copperfield's birthplace, 'Blunderstone', and at Bury St Edmunds the Angel Hotel commemorated his stay there by naming one of their rooms the Charles Dickens Room. The corruption and bribery that Dickens witnessed as a reporter in Suffolk during the 1836 general election was depicted in the famous Eatanswill election in *The Pickwick Papers*. The newspapers 'hoped' that there was to be no repetition of this sort in the trial of William Gardiner. The same newspaper editors later praised Henry Dickens, the only one of Charles's sons to make any mark on the world, for his 'moderate and balanced prosecution'.

Facing Henry Dickens was Mr Ernest Edward Wild (later Sir Ernest, Recorder of London), the son of a Norwich magistrate, who had an abiding interest in the theatre and as a consequence adopted a theatrical and flowing style in the courtroom. He was well built and distinguished-looking, a brilliant orator, and had one other unassailable advantage in a defence lawyer – he genuinely thought his client to be guiltless. He stayed with Gardiner's solicitor, Arthur Leighton, in Ipswich for the duration and both men were convinced of the defendant's innocence. Leighton made his name during the Gardiner trial and became adept at briefing the considerable press corps from local and national newspapers that dogged the court's every utterance.

On the third day of the trial the *East Anglian Daily Times* reported: 'Public interest was intensified when it became known that the prisoner himself would enter the witness box. The fair sex was again extensively represented in Court, and most of the females present had secured front places in the assembly – a fact which evoked some surprise.'

For four days Henry Dickens and Ernest Wild (whom, perhaps, some of the 'fair sex' came to view as much as the trial itself) turned over what in effect was purely circumstantial, if damning, evidence. The Crown could not prove that Gardiner had written the assignation note to Rose that would have placed him at the scene of the crime. It might have been written some weeks before the murder since it was not only unsigned but undated. In any case, Gardiner had an alibi in their immediate neighbour, the widowed Mrs Rose Ann Dickinson who kept an ironmonger's shop, from about half-past eleven, when the storm began, to around half-past one. Both he and his wife sat with the lately bereaved Mrs Dickinson who was frightened of the thunder and nervous of being in the house alone. Both women testified that Gardiner had been with them at midnight at the time that Mrs Crisp said she heard the thud and scream.

After exhaustive experiments at the chapel it was decided that the two young men who said they had listened to Gardiner and Rose together inside could barely have heard voices, let alone identify them conclusively. Gardiner's clothes and footwear were subjected to rigorous forensic testing to find either blood or paraffin, but neither was found. As to why there were no bloody footprints leading away from the scene it was suggested by Henry Dickens that the murderer must have removed his shoes to commit the crime! Handwriting experts were called to establish whether or not Gardiner had written either the assignation note or other letters found in her room, but there were conflicting views and no firm conclusions were reached. Under cross-examination, Mrs Crisp's story about hearing noises during the night of the murder, that would have undermined Gardiner's alibi, turned out to be imprecise and confused, and she was discredited as a witness. Mr Crisp, it transpired, was deaf.

The only evidence against Gardiner, it seemed, was his known association with Rose which, though he claimed it had ended, was thought by most people to have continued right up to the night of 31 May. He was surely the father of her baby and what better motive could there be for killing her?

In his summing up Mr Justice Grantham appeared to give a clear indication to the jury to return a guilty verdict. The following day some newspapers went so far as to say that his summing up was biased against Gardiner. The jury retired, only to return two hours later. What credence, they asked, should they give to the fact that no blood had been found on Gardiner's clothes and the lack of any evidence that he had destroyed either clothing or shoes? They were told that as far as they went the facts were in the prisoner's favour, but were by no means conclusive.

Some hours later they returned again but reported that there was an eleven-to-one majority and they were, therefore, unable to come to the required unanimous verdict. One juror had held out against an outright guilty verdict: Evan Edwards of Felixstowe, who was against capital punishment. The identity of the rogue juror was immediately leaked to the public and widely reported in the press. Mr Edwards wrote to the *East Anglian Daily Times* denying that he had been the odd man out, but it is certain that he was. Evan Edwards was an evangelical Christian, implacably opposed to the death penalty and well used to courting unpopularity. When the founder of the Salvation Army, General Booth, first visited Ipswich to open a new Mission it was Edwards who had accompanied the General through the streets. He shielded him against public opposition in more ways than once since the protests against the new Mission took the form of pelting the General with rotten fruit and eggs. Edwards might also have felt that Gardiner was being persecuted as a Nonconformist, and indeed there had been attempts to use his religious views against him. The longstanding rivalry between Nonconformists and the Church of England, where villages were split between church and chapel, was nowhere more pronounced than in Peasenhall and Sibton. Rose had attended the chapel but the rest of her family were churchgoers and made no secret of their belief in Gardiners' guilt, suggesting that the Methodist brethren were bound to defend one of their own.

Public reaction to the hung jury was contrary to expectation. Whereas Gardiner had until then been seen as the evildoer, he was now thought to have suffered an injustice. Some in the press began suggesting that Rose had not been entirely blameless in her demise and was certainly not the innocent maiden she was made out to be by the prosecution. It turned out that Gardiner was by no means the only man who could have been the father of her baby, and Rose's fiancé had broken off their engagement because of the scandal surrounding her name.

Georgianna Gardiner, who had six children to support, was bankrupted by the cost of the first trial and living on charity. She wrote to the *East Anglian Daily Times* pleading for help in financing the new trial. Her husband, she wrote, should have a proper defence. The paper opened a defence fund and Evan Edwards made a donation of £20. Many felt, as he did, that William Gardiner was being treated unfairly. A man was indeed entitled to a decent defence, especially when one trial had already failed to prove his guilt. Georgianna, whose loyalty to her husband never wavered, moved in with her sister in Ipswich so that she could visit him in prison.

For the second time, Mr Leighton employed the services of Ernest Wild, who took the unusual step of personally visiting Peasenhall where Mrs Crisp allowed them into Providence House. Henry Dickens KC was to prosecute a second time for the Crown.

On 21 January 1903 a new jury took its place under the direction of a new trial judge, Mr Justice Lawrence. The proceedings had been well publicised and media interest was frenzied. By then all the main players were known intimately to millions of readers and the national dailies sent their chief reporters to glean every sordid detail for their voracious readers. Ernest Wild feared that Gardiner would not get a fair trial in England, due to over-enthusiastic and hyperbolic press reporting. In his opening address Henry Dickens advised the jury to disregard everything they had read about the accused – difficult, if not impossible, advice.

The circumstantial evidence against William Gardiner was almost unchanged from that of the first trial and the witnesses were thoroughly rehearsed and rarely put a foot wrong. One of the young men who claimed to have heard William and Rose together in the chapel admitted that he had been reprimanded by Gardiner at work, but did not substantially alter his story.

Dr Charles Ryder Richardson, who had carried out the post mortem on Rose, described the wounds to her neck. Much to the delight of the reading public, he described numerous semi-circular cuts about her hands which were caused by warding off blows, thus putting paid once and for all to the ludicrous but persistent theory of suicide.

More handwriting experts were called to try to establish the identity of the writer of the assignation note. Thomas Gurrin was well known as an expert witness but under cross-examination his replies were less than conclusive. It was demonstrated that Gardiner had easy access to the buff-coloured envelopes and paper on which the note was written, as it was identical to that used in the Smyth offices, but not that he had actually written the note. Martha Walker, another expert in graphology, balanced the evidence by testifying in Gardiner's favour. Georgianna Gardiner gave evidence but fainted in court and was not able to go on. Reluctantly she returned later on the specific orders of Mr Justice Lawrence who decreed that hysteria ('high stericks' as the court heard it explained) was no excuse for her not to give evidence.

Finally Gardiner himself was called to the stand. Every detail of his association with Rose and the weeks surrounding her murder were gone over yet again. Consistently he denied murder and refuted all evidence to the contrary. He was asked about the incident in the Doctor's Chapel, as claimed by the two witnesses. 'It was compulsory then,' he said, 'for they could not go back from it. If they had done they would have been hooted from the place.' The prosecutor and the defence made their appeals and Mr Justice Lawrence gave his summing up after which, for the second time, a jury retired to decide the fate of William Gardiner. Was he the father of Rose's unborn child? Had he murdered her to prevent their secret being discovered and then tried to burn her body? How, though, had he managed to destroy what must have been severely blood-soaked clothing in the short time between leaving his house and joining his wife at Mrs Dickinson's?

Only two hours later the jury returned. The clerk asked the jury foreman, 'Are you agreed upon your verdict?' to which the reply came, 'No sir.' There was an audible murmur in court. Mr Justice Lawrence addressed the foreman, 'You are not agreed? Is there any chance of your agreeing?' 'No sir,' replied the foreman. For the second time there was an eleven-to-one hung jury. In the first trial only one juror thought him innocent. This time only one juror thought him guilty.

Gardiner was seen to lean forward as his wife collapsed in more 'high stericks'. The press corps sat poised on the edge of their seats. Was there to be a third trial?

Mr Justice Lawrence retired to his rooms and ordered that the prisoner be returned to gaol. Gardiner, and everyone else, must wait for his decision. Such was the pressure on the General Post Office from the national press that a team of Morse telegraph operators was sent from London to Ipswich to deal with the volume of words being sent to newspaper offices across the country. Almost unanimously the press deplored the injustice of leaving Gardiner in prison until the next Assizes in six months' time and suggested the case be heard at the Old Bailey. This would have the added advantage of easy access for the national dailies whose reporters were finding the journeys to and from Ipswich tedious. The *East Anglian Daily Times* reopened the defence fund and Evan Edwards again contributed the first £20. A London paper gathered a petition of 6,000 signatures demanding Gardiner's release and opened its own fund for Gardiner's family.

Five days later Mr Leighton received a telegram from the Director of Public Prosecutions. Gardiner would not be tried again. At the same time an order was sent to the governor of Ipswich Prison authorising his release. On hearing this news Gardiner is said to have dropped to his knees and thanked God for his deliverance. Messages of congratulation poured into the solicitor's office, Evan Edwards among the first to express support. Both William and Georgianna Gardiner gave independent interviews to the press and thanked those who had contributed to the defence funds; a theatre manager offered William £20 a week just to walk on the stage every night. A lecture organiser contacted them with an offer of a speaking tour.

Whatever they decided it was clear that the Gardiners could not return to Peasenhall. The mood there was very different to that in the rest of the country, where events had been seen through the romantic and sensationalist medium of the press. There were many villagers who thought him guilty and would have liked to see him hanged. (His job at the Drill Works had gone, strangely enough, to a man of the same name. Not only did a William Gardiner replace William Gardiner as foreman, but he also moved into his old home, Alma Cottage.) As time went on the myths and traditions of folk-lore attached themselves to the Gardiner family name: stories grew daily and stretched incredulity to the limit and were bandied about with no fear of retribution or restraint. William and Georgianna could not live in the same village as their reputation. Mr Leighton suggested that the Gardiners should take their children and start a new life in Canada, but they decided on Southall Green in London, where they took a corner shop. They had two more children but William no longer attended chapel. He died in 1941 and Georgianna, his loyal and stalwart companion, in 1948.

William Gardiner made no deathbed confession and throughout both trials, and thereafter, consistently maintained his innocence. There was only half an hour from the time his wife left to sit with the widowed Mrs Dickinson until William joined her there at about half-past eleven. During that interval he would have had to dash up to Providence House, argue with Rose and then kill her (having brought the knife, thus making it premeditated murder). Then he would have had to fetch newspaper and try to start a fire with a paraffin lamp, which would have left paraffin on his clothes and hands. He would then have had to change and dispose of the blood-soaked clothing and shoes, wash the blood off, get rid of the smell of paraffin and arrive at Mrs Dickinson's as though nothing had happened. Georgianna might have been a dutiful wife, but she was also a devout and ardent Primitive Methodist. It is difficult to think that if she had any suspicions about William's guilt she would not have betrayed them to the court under cross-examination. It was suggested during the trial that there had been a bonfire in the Gardiners' yard early on Sunday morning, the day after the murder, but if William had destroyed a jacket or other clothing, the prudent and frugal Georgianna would undoubtedly have known.

But if William Gardiner did not murder Rose Harsent, who did? There were several false confessions, including that of an ex-soldier who said he broke into the house and killed her on impulse. But this was discounted after police inquiries. Today, using advanced forensic tests, it would be possible not only to determine if Rose's blood had been on any of Gardiner's clothing, but also the paternity of her baby and thus throw better light on a possible second suspect. But all this took place when forensic science was in its infancy. If Gardiner had been found guilty at his first trial he would, under the majority verdict rule, have been hanged and there would have been no second trial.

Another possibility is that William Harsent, at odds with Rose over her attendance at the chapel instead of the church, and about her 'reputation' in the village, struck her in anger on discovering that she was pregnant. Like Gardiner he was a countryman and was likely to carry the same kind of knife as he did, and either of them could have taken a knife from the kitchen – the murder weapon was never identified. Given the public knowledge of her liaison with Gardiner he could have attempted to frame him. He was certainly in a position to know all the details of the alleged affair and would not have approved or condoned such goings on. When asked in court if he thought his daughter likely to commit suicide he replied: 'No I have not seen anything in her to suggest that.' No one asked him if he had struck Rose. He did, though, inform the Coroner that Rose's life was insured by the Prudential and presumably, as her next of kin, he was entitled to any payout.

Rumour and theory abound to this day in Peasenhall. It is said that at Providence House, darkening can still be seen on the floor where Rose was murdered and where her blood seeped into the porous bricks at the foot of the staircase that led to the attic bedroom.

Her ghost is said to haunt both Providence House and the old Doctor's Chapel, which can still be seen behind what was once the home of Dr Lay. Rose herself lies in the graveyard of St Michael's Church in Peasenhall. No one was ever convicted of her murder.

NINE

Murder at the Red Barn

FOR ALMOST TWO hundred years the extraordinary story of William Corder and Maria Marten has been Suffolk's most notorious tale of murder and intrigue. It is not so much the murder itself – there have been plenty of those over the centuries – or even the dissection of whether or not he committed the deed, since he made a full and frank confession of all that happened. Rather, it is the actual dissection of William Corder's body that compels such macabre fascination and the fact that ten thousand people thronged the prison to witness his execution and anatomisation. It is still possible to see Corder's scalp with one ear attached at Moyse's Hall Museum in Bury St Edmunds, together with a book bound in the killer's skin that tells the story of his crime. His skeleton is held at the Royal College of Surgeons in London. No wonder that in 2002 a relative of William Corder asked that all the parts of his body be returned to the family for Christian burial.

On 18 May 1827 twenty-six-year-old Maria Marten left her thatched cottage in the village of Polstead, just north of Stoke-by-Nayland, and set out to meet her lover. She was a good-looking girl, educated and gregarious, with high hopes of making a favourable marriage with William Corder, the twenty-four-year-old son of local farmer John Corder. The Corder family had done well out of agriculture and held the tenancy on 300 acres. Although at school his nickname was 'Foxey', because he was given to stealing and lying, William was young, respectable and well off – an advantageous union for the daughter of mole-catcher Thomas Marten.

The rendezvous was the Red Barn, on the Corder estate where Maria hoped to make her home, William having promised to marry her. The Marten family considered that something of a duty rested on William's shoulders since his older brother had already seduced Maria but deserted her when she had his child (who later died). Maria's tryst with William on that Friday had special significance: she was sure that this time he would honour his promise and she could begin her new life as Mrs William Corder. William's father and brother had died in the February and he had recently taken over the farm. She knew that William's mother Mary far from approved of her as a daughter-in-law, which was hardly surprising since she had not only had a child by William's brother, but also a son by another local landowner, Peter Matthews. William suggested, therefore, that they go to Ipswich to be married so that his mother would not know until it was too late. Furthermore, he told her to dress as a man so that anyone seeing them leave Polstead together would not recognise her.

They also shared a secret that Maria thought would bind William to her side. In the very same month that William's father John had died she had left her older son at Polstead with her father and went to lodgings in Sudbury, where she gave birth to William's child. But the infant died shortly after Maria returned home and William decided that the birth should be kept secret. He persuaded Maria to put the dead baby in a cardboard box and bury it in a field. This would have a twofold advantage in that his mother need not know about the baby, and Maria's hold over him would lessen.

As she approached the Corders' farm on a bright and cloudless May morning, Maria Marten hurried as best she could. Her several layers of clothes hampered her progress but if it meant getting safely to Ipswich it would be worthwhile. She arrived at the Red Barn somewhat breathless and rather hot, but in a state of excited anticipation.

That evening, Maria's family thought it peculiar that she failed to return home, especially as she was very attached to her young son, but assumed that William had at last made good his promise to take her to Ipswich and made an 'honest' woman of her. Two days later Maria's stepmother saw William in Polstead. Where, she asked, was Maria? He explained that he had left Maria in Ipswich but that she was going to visit a friend at the seaside before returning. The Marten family was puzzled but there was nothing they could do. For the next five months William continued running the farm and successfully fended off Thomas Marten's daily enquiries as to the health and whereabouts of his daughter.

Finally, at the end of September, William called on Thomas Marten. He was, he said, going to London where he had arranged to meet Maria and where they would be married. Leaving his mother to run the farm he took £400 and went first to the Isle of Wight, apparently for a holiday, and then to London. He wrote to Thomas informing him that he and Maria were man and wife. He went on to ask why Thomas had not replied to Maria's letters. Because, answered Thomas, no letters had arrived. He asked William for money to help look after Maria's son, Thomas Henry. A sovereign arrived at the mole-catcher's cottage with William's reply, in which he expressed further surprise that Thomas had still not answered Maria's letters.

By April 1828, the Marten family had not seen Maria for almost a year. They were told she was Mrs William Corder but she had sent no word to her son and the manner of her departure was still unexplained. It was then that Mrs Marten began to have strange dreams. She told her husband that she dreamed Maria was in the Red Barn and that he should go there and find her.

Somewhat unwillingly Thomas Marten and the local bailiff broke into the Red Barn. He had with him his mole spike, which he prodded into the barn floor. Horrified he saw that clinging to the spike was what appeared to be putrid flesh. Thomas realised that his daughter had never been in Ipswich, or London. She had never left Polstead, nor was she married, but instead lay dead, buried in the floor of the Red Barn. Thomas Marten was in no doubt who the murderer was.

After leaving Polstead, William had in fact first visited a health spa, spent some time on the Isle of Wight, and then went to London. There he decided he would advertise for a wife. One of the ninety-five replies that he received was, by coincidence, from Mary Moore, a young woman whom he had met in the Isle of Wight. William and Mary fell passionately in love and were married within the week. They moved in with Mary's mother and opened a girls' school, to all intents and purposes a happy and perfectly normal married couple.

Four days after Maria's body was discovered, Suffolk police went to arrest Corder. They brought him back to Polstead in the early hours of 25 April where he had to run the gauntlet of the final stages of the inquest, being held at the Cock Inn. Villagers and strangers came to join in the proceedings and hear the grisly details of Maria's final demise. She had been strangled, stabbed and shot, and had sustained injury to her head. The press went into overdrive and from a barrage of one-sided, hyped-up reporting emerged new and sensational 'facts' from which there emerged an indelible folk tale.

Evidence was given by a succession of witnesses, all of whom incriminated Corder beyond doubt. His scarf was found on the body . . . he possessed a small sword that fitted the stab wounds . . . he had a pistol . . . he had lied about Maria's whereabouts for a year . . . and he had been her lover and father of her child, whose body had been disposed of in suspicious circumstances. When arrested he was also in possession of Maria's bag, though at the time he denied knowing anyone called Maria Marten. Maria's young half-brother testified that on the day of the murder he saw the accused go to the Red Barn carrying a pickaxe.

William Corder was formally arrested and committed to Bury St Edmunds gaol to await the next Suffolk Assizes, held at Shire Hall, Bury St Edmunds, during August 1828. Because of Corder's notoriety huge numbers of people wanted places in the public gallery and local hotel-keepers doubled their prices to take advantage of those needing lodging. Because of the nature of the trial women were barred and eventually only men issued with tickets could gain admission.

The start of the trial was delayed as the judge and members of the court took almost an hour to fight their way through the crowds to get into Shire Hall. Several thousand of those without tickets collected outside and were fed information by those within. Maria's decomposing head was used as evidence in the trial and throughout William maintained his innocence.

William's wife was allowed to visit him in gaol, bringing what comfort she could. When not at the prison, or engaged in consultation with the solicitor charged with her husband's defence, she was in Polstead supporting her mother-in-law. William would not allow his mother to visit the prison, knowing it would distress her.

After two days the jury found Corder guilty. He was sentenced to be hanged and his body given to medical research. As the judge, Chief Baron Alexander, passed sentence Corder collapsed and was led sobbing back to gaol. So hopeful was his wife that he would be released, she had ordered a chaise to take him home. His mother and wife were united in their grief and shock that so much of the trial had come from the prosecution and almost nothing in William's defence. No plea of manslaughter was raised, and far from being portrayed as a 'scarlet woman', who had three bastard children by as many men, Maria Marten's reputation was not seriously called into question.

Eventually, persuaded by his wife, William made a full confession, though he always denied the stabbing and said that he had not intended to kill Maria but there was an argument and the pistol had gone off by accident.

William Corder was hanged three days after his trial, before ten thousand people. Despite the pouring rain the crowd thronged the county gaol to witness the hanging, some having travelled from London. Afterwards the body was taken to the Shire Hall, where it was cut open from throat to abdomen and laid out on show. Men and women filed past to view it before it was removed for dissection to the West Suffolk Hospital. The hangman claimed the trousers and stockings as a 'matter of right'. The surgeon, George Creed, later had an account of the trial bound in leather made from Corder's skin.

One of the star attractions at Moyse's Hall Museum in Bury St Edmunds is a copy of Corder's death bust where the marks of the hangman's rope are clearly visible round his throat. It was made by Mr Child of Bungay, who sent a copy to a noted phrenologist, Dr Spurzheim, who 'read' its bumps; he found Corder 'sadly lacking in morality'.

Did William Corder murder Maria Marten? It is fairly certain that he did, but it was more likely to have been in anger and as a result of Maria's provocation, rather than premeditated murder. He was certainly a liar and a cheat, but after his marriage he appeared to have changed. His relationship with his wife shows him to have been loving and considerate of both her and his mother. He wrote a letter to his wife, delivered by the Revd Stocking on the day of the hanging, in which he called her 'My life's loved Companion'. He called on Heaven to bless and protect her through 'this transitory vale of misery' and that they would meet again 'in the regions of bliss'. His last prayer was that God would grant her patience, fortitude and resignation. Mary was to need fortitude and more besides as she was pregnant and gave birth to Corder's child a few months after his death.

And what of Maria's stepmother? There were rumours later that she and Corder were lovers and that she knew about the murder but kept quiet until she heard that he had married. A woman scorned is a dangerous enemy. Ann Marten's apparent dreams began in mid-December 1827, only days after Corder married. Perhaps she knew about the mysterious circumstances in which he and Maria buried their child, and had blackmailed him into a relationship with her. William was suspected of having poisoned the child to avoid a scandal and forestall his marriage to Maria. Suggestions were also made that Maria herself was blackmailing him over the fate of their child and that the price of her silence was marriage.

Was 'Foxey' Corder, then, a black-hearted villain destined to die on the gallows, and deservedly so? Whatever the rights and wrongs of the case it is absolutely certain that the trial was press-driven and a travesty of justice. By his own admission they had quarrelled and he had shot her, but was he the monster he was made out to be by the prosecution? There is more than a suspicion that the police added charges of stabbing and throttling for good measure, to be sure of a conviction. If the thousands congregated in Bury to witness a hanging had been disappointed there could have been a riot.

The industry surrounding the Red Barn murder has not abated over the years and what passed for gossip in 1828 quickly became fact. A ballad based on the murder was composed soon after Corder's execution, and the broadsheets of the time published innumerable versions of the events. The rope used to hang Corder was sold off by the hangman at a guinea an inch.

At the start of the twentieth century film took over from the numerous books and articles written over the years. In 1913 Maurice Elvey's *Maria Marten* was filmed on location at Polstead, and in 1935 the director Milton Rosmer made the famous *Murder in the Red Barn* for MGM, starring Todd Slaughter and Hilary Eaves.

Until the 1940s nurses at the West Suffolk Hospital were taught anatomy with Corder's skeleton and they even used to sneak him out with them to dances. It is also said that donations totalling about £50 a year were raised for charity by rigging the skeleton up to a loose floorboard which, when stepped on, would cause Corder to raise an arm.

After sentence Corder is said to have accepted his fate but was distraught at hearing that his body was to be anatomised. He exclaimed to the prison governor, 'Oh, God! Nobody will dig my grave!'

Is it possible that William Corder will at least have a belated Christian ceremony of committal? A spokeswoman for the Royal College of Surgeons told the *East Anglian Daily Times* in July 2002 that Corder's skeleton had been taken off display. If, eventually, the skeleton is disposed of, it will most likely be cremated and not buried, to avoid it becoming a site of ghoulish interest. This might draw a line under one aspect of this long-running tale, but it is unlikely to diminish the continuing interest in William Corder and the Red Barn murder.

TEN

The war against tithe

FROM TIME IMMEMORIAL farming and various denominations of the church held parallel sway in Suffolk, for better or for worse and for richer or for poorer. The tithe, or tenth part of personal income, went towards the upkeep of the clergy and was originally paid by everyone. Until 1836, farming tithes were calculated in produce, rather than cash, and other 'personal' tithes all but disappeared. The tenth pig was the parson's pig, a tenth of the hay and corn crops, the tenth pint of milk, and so on. Liability to tithe was once tied to all land, but over time, especially after the Reformation, when Henry VIII split from the Church of Rome and set up the Church of England, it applied to some land, not all. In Suffolk, because of its fertile corn-growing nature, agricultural tithe was widespread and very high.

Although the population drift from country to town had already begun by the middle of the eighteenth century, at the start of the twentieth century most people still living in the countryside were involved with farming and either the church or the chapel. Even those living in the towns often still had some familial links with the rural areas, especially in predominantly rural counties like Suffolk. Unlike today, those who lived in the countryside were connected with agriculture through employment or trade, but until the First World War there were very few small farmers or independent owner-occupiers. The majority of farms were tenanted and the huge estates, which often encompassed numerous parishes, operated tenant–landlord arrangements that owed their existence to dynasty builders of the eighteenth and nineteenth centuries who used their country seats to consolidate their positions in society. These estate owners traditionally carried the responsibility for tithe as part of their subscription to the higher echelons of the established order. Once the Church of England became the Established Church, so it became the church of the establishment, and there were few more enthusiastic members of it than the large estate owners and those who farmed the heavily productive arable acres of Suffolk.

In 1918, however, just when farming profits were the highest they had been since before the Napoleonic wars, the estate owners saw an opportunity to rid themselves of unwanted land at inflated, and they knew short-lived, prices. Many had lost money in the war and they knew that current returns would only be temporary. Once imports (severely reduced during the war) resumed, agriculture would slip back into its customary state of depression. Weighed down by crippling death duties, and loss of income from outside investments, the estate owners began to sell parcels of land. Over the next few years vast tracts of the British countryside changed hands and between 1918 and 1920 almost one-tenth of agricultural land was bought by tenants.

It was this army of 'new' owner-occupiers who were to experience the dramatic post-war decrease in farm prices. Hardly were they home from the bank, mortgaged to the hilt but buoyed up by post-war euphoria, than the government withdrew most of the support measures that had prevailed for the duration of the war. By 1923 farming was in such straits that the agricultural wage was forced down to 25 shillings a week and profit margins shrank almost to nothing. As if that was not enough, it came as something of a shock to these new farmers, now struggling to pay their mortgages, to find that their farms were not entirely their own. Something called tithe was payable to their local clergyman, or to some institution or distant person, who had a tenth share in their land. Not all farms paid it, either, which was doubly puzzling, and it had something to do with Queen Anne who died in 1714.

On enquiry they were referred to the 1918 Tithe Act but searched their farm particulars in vain for any mention of the Church of England, Queen Anne or indeed tithe itself. It was not then compulsory for the vendor to mention tithe in the sale catalogue. An invoice demanding a sum of 'rentcharge' was sometimes the first hint of their liability. In the years to come much was to be made of the fact that owner-occupiers had bought their land knowing that it was subject to tithe, but in fact many bought from unscrupulous vendors who wanted full market price for the land, without any deductions.

By 1924 a strong anti-tithe movement had formed, the impetus coming from the combined efforts of East Anglian, Kentish and Welsh farmers. More than 100,000 farmers across England and Wales (tithe no longer existed anywhere else in the world) began the long fight to end tithe. With Suffolk's deeply entrenched Nonconformists now having to pay tithe to the Church of England, the leaders of what became known as the 'tithe war' emerged from its ranks. Doreen Wallace, a Scot married to a Suffolk farmer, lent her name and reputation as a best-selling novelist; Philip Butler was a farmer at Barking, near Needham Market, who was also a Quaker, a poet and an artist; the Turner family from Elmsett who, though members of the Church of England, fought on the side of the tithepayers; and Lady Eve Balfour, who played a leading role as both recalcitrant tithepayer and supporter.

Men and women from all levels of society weighed in and did their bit, but head and shoulders above them all was a Suffolk farmer from Oulton, Albert George Mobbs (1887–1978) who first began his fight against tithe in 1924 and continued the struggle for sixty years. Besides devoting astounding amounts of time and effort to organising and supporting the tithepayers' revolt, not just in Suffolk but across England and Wales, A.G. (as he was universally known) was also a successful farmer, lifelong member of the National Farmers Union and churchman. He was also a local councillor, once sharing a political platform with David Lloyd George, and worked tirelessly on behalf of tithepayers, attending meetings, organising sales, writing letters to the editor and giving press and radio interviews.

A. G. Mobbs was born into the highest ideals of Methodism, his parents and grandparents steeped in the most solid kind of political ambition there is – that born out of duty and concern for the common man and not self-aggrandisement. His grandfather was William Mobbs, the butcher of Tonning Street, Lowestoft, dubbed the 'butcher with the heart of gold' (who we will meet in Chapter 15). The twin weapons of Nonconformity and political Liberalism combined to make A. G. the perfect vehicle for dissent. His ingrained sense of justice, and what constituted social injustice, was aroused by the arbitrary and archaic tithe and, having discovered its nature, he resolved that the taxation of a minority for the maintenance of an Established Church was wrong and must be opposed.

In his unpublished autobiography he wrote:

> In 1926 I found myself concentrating on an outstanding injustice which appeared to have no justification whatsoever, namely the enforcing of tithe demands. Things began to move fairly rapidly, particularly in the Kent area where they had a hop tithe of around £1 per acre. They had already started a National Tithepayers' Association (NTA), which I joined in the early stages.

Unsurprisingly, the Church of England and the 'lay' impropriators, that is, non-church owners such as universities, institutions and individuals who held entitlement to tithe income, united to defend both their rights to tithe and to force payment through the courts. The main body charged with extracting the money was Queen Anne's Bounty (QAB) and from 1930 onwards it was the declared intention of the tithepayers to fight for the abolition of tithe, while

QAB had no choice: it had to uphold the law and get the money by whatever means possible.

By 1931 it was obvious to many in Suffolk that they needed to be better organised, so A. G. Mobbs arranged a meeting at the Crown and Anchor Hotel, Ipswich in the February of that year. He wrote:

> [It] was advertised as being for the purpose of forming a Suffolk Tithepayers' Association (TPA). We were crowded out, a large number of farmers being unable to obtain admission. We soon agreed to set up an organisation with myself as Chairman and Mr Makens Turners, another member of the Suffolk National Farmers Union executive, as Vice Chairman. We had already contacted a Mr Philip Butler, who had been seen in Ipswich carrying sandwich boards, which called public attention to the unjust tithe demands.

Philip Butler belonged to the Quakers, a religious body for whose members special laws were at one time enacted enabling authorities to fine and imprison those who defaulted on tithe payments. He was, wrote A.G., 'a man of outstanding integrity and became a very popular and efficient secretary'.

At the same meeting Doreen Wallace (1897–1989) made herself known to a Suffolk audience for the first time. Born in Cumbria of Scottish parents, she gained an honours degree at Oxford University, after which she taught in a secondary school in Diss before marrying Rowland Rash, a farmer at Wortham on the Norfolk–Suffolk border. She revelled in the cause and took up the challenge with a flourish, using her novels to make political points and her name as a writer (of nearly fifty books) to attract the all-important publicity the Suffolk TPA needed. Doreen and A.G. were from very different backgrounds but they made a formidable team. She was fired with the same sense of injustice (there was no tithe in Scotland, she pointed out) but approached the subject with a trained mind that understood the incredibly complicated tithe history and could transmit the essentials to the foot-soldiers of the campaign. In 1933 she wrote in the foreword to *The Tithe War*:

> My little book records the biased observations of a tithepayer

under notice of distraint. I make no claim to omniscience, broad-mindedness, or even good temper; I have, however, about as much of each of these desirable qualities as any titheowner with whom I have yet come into contact. I have, in addition, a grievance, for I am experiencing the oppression of the Tithe Laws. And I have an inspiration: the courage and conviction of my fellow soldiers in the Tithe War.

Doreen and A.G. were both excellent, charismatic public speakers, both tall and commanding in stature, and able to hold an audience's attention by their ability to relate dry facts accurately, but simply, and with impact. A.G. never addressed a meeting without a practice run-through backed by meticulous, some might say pedantic, research. His wife Dorothy supported him in his crusade, although her interest in tithe was, unlike her husband's, finite. She under-standably became tired of the subject, and A.G.'s habit of rehearsing his countless speeches meant hours as a one-woman audience. Dorothy Mobbs was, though, deaf in one ear, and would indul-gently 'listen' to the speech with a book in one hand and a finger in the good ear. To A.G.'s 'What did you think of that, dear?' she would smile and say, 'Very good, dear!'

A.G. and Doreen Wallace had an intense but entirely respectable and businesslike relationship that often called for impromptu meetings. On one occasion a widow had seen her crops and machinery sold to pay her tithe and A.G. decided that the Suffolk TPA must help out. He wrote:

I rang Mrs Rash in the morning, which was market day, and requested her to meet me at Ipswich. I was convinced we could collect sufficient to compensate the widow for her loss by asking for donations. When I phoned her and told her of my plans she replied 'Oh, A.G.,' (that is what they called me) 'I'm sorry but I'm having a tennis party here this afternoon.'

Almost immediately she changed her mind and decided that the tennis party could wait. She rang back to ask, 'Where shall I meet you?' It was arranged that Doreen should first visit the Corn Exchange and A.G. would go to the Cattle Market. Then, wrote A.G.:

We met for tea at Limmers in the Butter Market and cashed up. Her bag and my pockets were bulging with notes and cash, which we emptied onto the tea table. Folks around must have thought we had just robbed a bank! Anyhow, the sum total was nearly £100 and I wrote out a cheque sufficient to cover the loss of the corn crop, which the widow received next morning.

Once formal opposition got under way the committee decided that the first thing that the new Suffolk TPA needed was a show-piece court case for the press to get their teeth into that would bring the matter to the public's attention. The case of Jones versus Mrs I. M. Sullivan was just what was needed and had the advantage of involving a 'lay' impropriator and not the Church.

Mr Jones had emigrated to Australia but returned to England in 1929 with his Australian-born wife and bought a 750-acre unit of land, comprising separate farms, from the Stoke College Estate near Sudbury, which he renamed 'Australia Farms'. Mr Jones paid his first tithe demand, a half-yearly payment assessed at 6 shillings an acre, without quite knowing why. He was not unduly bothered, as he thought he was going into a profitable farming enterprise. Instead he was part of the 'slump' of the 1930s and his income fell dramatically. Food imports continued to increase while other importing countries closed their frontiers in order to protect their own farmers. Overall profits fell away and wheat prices plummeted from 46 shillings a quarter to 22 shillings, but Mrs Sullivan could not only demand over £200 a year regardless of his ability to pay but she could also legally seize farm stock for non-payment. A.G. wrote:

Mr Jones told us he had received a court order for distraint on his goods, and was prepared to allow the law to take its course if we would support him. This turned out to be our first tithe sale in the county, an announcement of which appeared in the *East Anglian Daily Times*. I at once contacted that paper and told them I wanted to advertise a protest meeting by our Association to take place immediately after the sale of Mr Jones's goods and asked that it might appear on the same page, directly under the sale notice.

The sale of Mr Jones's goods by order of the court, to pay his outstanding tithe debts, went ahead and set a pattern devised by the Suffolk TPA which was to be carried out in thousands of similar circumstances over the next few years. No bids were made for any of the goods, except low and derisory amounts proffered by A. G. Mobbs himself. By this method, the sale took its legal course, but the titheowner got very little of the money. The court orders were, therefore, carried out in their legal entirety but gave only a small return to the titheowner while the tithepayer, whose goods were sold, did not go home empty-handed as the goods were returned to him.

The auctioneer pointed out a potential problem with this scam. He told A.G. that he could not see that he had assisted the farmer because, no doubt, the goods would be returned and possibly distrained on again. A.G. replied: 'I have no intention of giving the goods back. They are mine and I intend to lend them to Mr Jones for the rest of his life!' He then appealed to the farmers to let the auctioneer leave quietly and they proceeded with the protest meeting. Such meetings followed almost all distraint sales, and in April 1933 the first of the 'Gift Sales' took place in Ipswich. Well-wishers and TPA members donated stock which was auctioned, the proceeds going towards the Suffolk TPA funds. Money could then be used to help tithepayers in financial distress. Doreen Wallace wrote:

> The quantity of miscellaneous goods for sale was so great that three auctioneers were kept at work selling simultaneously from two o'clock in the afternoon till late evening; the lots ranged from first-class dairy heifers and well-fed calves and pigs down to parcels of half a dozen eggs from smallholders who could afford no more. Men whose farms were denuded of stock sent implements, tumbrils, corn, potatoes, or mangolds; there were many gifts of poultry; and sympathisers who were not farmers sent joints of meat, sides of bacon, and even clothing.

Inevitably, as the tithe gatherings became high-profile news, the movement attracted the attention of fringe political elements. Far and away the most potentially dangerous were the followers of

Sir Oswald Mosley (1896–1980) who began to turn up at what during the 1930s became the almost daily scenes of distraint mayhem. Attracted by a thousand or more angry farmers and the accompanying press corps, the resultant coverage began to favour them, rather than the tithepayers. It became essential that the association between the farming community and the British Union of Fascists (BUF) be halted in its tracks. While it was true that Mosley was the only politician to offer any kind of farming policy in the inter-war years, no one in the Suffolk TPA or National Tithepayers' Association (NTA) – especially A. G. Mobbs – wanted their cause contaminated by association with the BUF or fascist violence.

The Blackshirt involvement reached a climax in 1934 when Doreen and Rowland Rash were distrained upon for non-payment of tithe. Stock valued at £702 was impounded at their Suffolk farm and hundreds of farmers came from all over the county to help 'defend' the stock from the bailiffs. Blackshirts, too, arrived and the local police sent for reinforcements. Large numbers of people converged on Wortham over several days – fascists, police, tithepayers' associations from all over the country, families and friends of the Suffolk TPA, and well-wishers and supporters of the Rash family. The Blackshirts were eventually arrested and returned to London and while a game of cat and mouse was played out between the bailiffs and the Rashes, no one was hurt and the expected violence did not materialise. Although for the TPA leaders those were anxious times, many remembered the events as some of the most exciting days of their lives. Nothing quite so dramatic had happened in that part of Suffolk for many years.

Later that year Oswald Mosley himself came to Ipswich, a visit designed to coincide with the presence in the town of the (then) peripatetic Royal Show. He repeated his message of Britain being the dumping-ground for cheap foreign goods that undercut the British farmer. He spoke at a dinner given in Ipswich and, while he espoused sentiments guaranteed to find favour in rural Suffolk, the mood was open-minded but guarded. At the end of the meeting many of the farmers present found themselves standing and answering Mosley's fascist salute, but only a year after they had listened so attentively to his message they became uncomfortably aware of his hidden agenda and rejected all association with the BUF.

After four long years of acrimonious exchanges between tithe-payers and the authorities the government announced a Royal Commission to look into the whole matter of tithe. It sat for eighteen months and the resultant recommendations, when they came, plunged the NTA leaders into despair. It had forty-three clauses and nine schedules, which changed the character of tithe without releasing landowners from blatantly unfair and divisive liabilities that made the Church of England their enemy. Far from recommending its immediate abolition, which had been the single aim of the tithepayers, it acknowledged the unsatisfactory state of tithe as it existed, reluctantly agreeing to its final demise, but suggesting a redemption period of forty years. The Tithe Bill extended this to sixty years, thus carrying the problem of tithe on until 1996.

On a stifling day in June 1936, 5,000 men and women from all over the country left their farms – at no small cost, since it was haymaking time – to take part in a huge march on London. They arrived in private cars and carts, sixteen special trains and hundreds of coaches. Hundreds of farmers, their families, and farm workers left Suffolk to join the march from Victoria Embankment to Hyde Park. A. G. Mobbs, Doreen Wallace and Lady Eve Balfour were among those who addressed the crowds to demand the withdrawal of the Tithe Bill.

For the tithepayers it was their finest hour. They could not have done better: in publicity terms it was a triumph. That night it was shown on the Pathe News and Doreen Wallace, standing on platform three, made a particularly dramatic figure as she exhorted the crowds to push for a new Tithe Bill and lobby their MPs accordingly. A casualty of the day, though, was Doreen's friendship with her fellow author Dorothy L. Sayers who, from her seat in a cinema, saw her old Somerville crony 'bawling from a farm wagon' in Hyde Park and was not impressed. The two had met at Oxford and had forged a close friendship, but for Sayers – a parson's daughter educated on the proceeds of tithe income – it ended their relationship.

In 1937 A. G. Mobbs became President of the National Tithepayers' Association. His indomitable spirit had inspired its members through protest after protest and continued to lead them in despair after the government forced through the 1936 Tithe Act.

Despite considerable opposition by 130 MPs the Bill received royal assent in the autumn of 1936. The Liberal MP for the Eye Division, Edgar Granville (1898–1998) was one of those who opposed it. Elected in 1929 he remained in the House of Commons until 1951 and was a stalwart supporter of the Suffolk TPA. As a parliamentary private secretary he was widely expected to resign, but it was appreciated that he had no alternative but to vote against the government. He could not support legislation that would compel a large number of his constituents to pay tithe (or rentcharge, as it had been renamed) for another sixty years. Every country in the world had by then abolished tithe except England and Wales, where it was to remain a burden for at least another generation.

A. G. Mobbs wrote:

> The ultimate effect of the Bill was that as a result of the absolutely disgraceful intervention of the Archbishop, Parliament took over the responsibility of buying out the tithe recipients by a form of compensation equivalent to a capital sum of over £70 million, with the tithepayers having to make good that sum by annual payments until 1996, by which date the 'ransom' money would cease to be paid and freedom bought from an age-long wrong by those whose only crime was that they chose as their form of livelihood the growing of food for their fellow human beings.

Archbishop Cosmo Lang had indeed intervened and by doing so added to the distress not only of the tithepayers but also those clergy who thought that they ought to be paid by their Church and not by money extracted from unwilling contributors. The plight of the rural clergy was no less acute than that of their farming neighbours and many were embarrassed at having to rely on an arbitrary system of income, which set them at odds with their parishioners. The Church was by no means the only titheholder, but it was the largest and was expected to take a higher moral stand on the issue than, say, the universities.

Other sections of the community were similarly adversely affected. Auctioneers invariably found themselves having to auction off a client's assets for tithe, while the law itself came into disrepute. One of the most high-profile judges was Alfred Hildesley, KC (1873–1958), who became a County Court judge on the Suffolk and Essex circuit in 1931 and chairman of the East Suffolk Quarter Session. Due to the phenomenal number of tithe cases that came before his court he was dubbed 'the Tithe Judge'.

Judge Hildesley had been one of the few barristers of his time who was familiar with ecclesiastical law, which was the reason for his appointment. He lived at Onehouse Lodge, near Stowmarket, and however sympathetic he may have been towards the farmers he remained calm and implacable in the face of demonstrations both in court and outside. He made it plain that he was there to enforce the law as it stood. He told a lady tithepayer at Halesworth County Court that whether she could afford to pay or not, the money was due by law and he could not be swayed by claims of destitution or poverty: 'I hear these things in seventeen different Courts. I have nothing to do with meetings or bodies of titheowners or tithepayers. Each case is dealt with individually. In this case the husband has the means to pay, and an order will be made.' The judge's daughter, Elizabeth, who kept house for her father and brothers at Onehouse, wrote: 'At least one local farmer tried bribery and sent goods to Onehouse Lodge. These were, of course, returned to him immediately and had no effect.'

The main courts were at Ipswich, Bury St Edmunds and Colchester, with lesser ones scattered round the county, so Judge Hildesley came to know Suffolk very well. The family joined in the social life of the county and the judge's youngest son later held a commission in the Suffolk Regiment. Although he rarely showed favouritism within the law he admitted to a profound sense of sympathy with the rural clergy. Elizabeth remembers that her father had a wonderful memory for names and people, and was a genial host:

A number of clergy attended our parties, some of them in very poor circumstances due to unpaid tithe. In those days there were no diocesan scales for clergy stipends, the money deriving from former benefactions, the Easter Offering, tithe and sometimes a generous patron or squire. Pensions were very small and most clergy had no chance of saving towards a house for retirement, unless they had private means, so they remained at work often until they died, living in very large vicarages which they could not afford to heat except minimally. The Judge was aware of this situation and very sympathetic.

During the Second World War the judge moved to Bury St Edmunds and when he died in 1958 in his eighty-fifth year, all the obituaries referred to 'the Tithe Judge' who had dealt with the numerous cases arising out of the tithe war with a measure of tact and discretion that did much to reduce the heat of the situation.

Even during the Second World War, when home food production was of national importance, the Tithe Redemption Commission went about its business. A. G. Mobbs continued to receive letters from distressed tithepayers and he continued to withhold rentcharge payments due on his own farm at Oulton, forcing the Commission to take him to court for every penny. In 1964 the Tithe Redemption Office offered him the opportunity to extinguish his liability for £658 17s. 10d., but he refused and once more found himself in front of the bench at Lowestoft Magistrates Court.

A. G. Mobbs was ninety years old when in October 1977 he paid his final tithe demand of £87.28. The previous year the Inland Revenue had finally tired of pursuing tithepayers for what had become derisory sums of money which were costing more to collect than they were worth. Lady Eve Balfour, Doreen Wallace and Rowland Rash also lived to see the end of tithe, though Rowland died in 1977 only a few weeks after it ended. They and the thousands of other tithepayers were the last of a dying breed; men and women of ordinary means whose strength of conviction gave them the courage to take on the Establishment in times when unquestioned deference and automatic respect for one's 'elders and betters' ruled supreme. They learned to rise above the intensity of their anger and frustration whilst maintaining a burning, unquenchable sense of injustice.

There are two permanent reminders of the tithe war in Suffolk. At Elmsett, parishioners walk and drive past the Tithe Memorial daily. It is sited opposite the church entrance as a visible reminder of the harsh, dark days of the 1930s when the Westren family's goods were sold to pay their dues.

The monument at Wortham is now covered with lichen and stands on a bank beside the site of the Rash's farmyard where the Blackshirts once lined up to do battle with the police and where, finally, cattle and pigs were seized by the bailiffs and sold for tithe. It was unveiled in 1935 by Dorothy Mobbs and is there to remind those who seek it out of the days when a man's goods could be taken by force by the state to pay the clergy, regardless of the circumstances of the payer.

Although agricultural tithe was finally redeemed in 1977 a part of it lives on in the form of the Chancel Repairs Act 1932, which is still on the statute books. It allowed the Church to demand money from the titleholders of ancient 'rights' that for almost two thousand years tied the community to their church. In 1994 the Church of England tested this right in the courts and, unbelievably, the landowners heard parts of the sixteenth-century Act of Succession read out in court.

In 2001 the courage and validity of the tithepayers, who fought so valiantly for abolition throughout the 1930s and 1940s, was vindicated. The European Convention on Human Rights concluded that the liability of lay owners of what was once the glebe land of a rectory to defray the cost of chancel repairs was a form of taxation that did not meet the basic standards. It operated 'arbitrarily' and was unjustified.

How those protagonists of the Suffolk TPAs would have devoured the words 'arbitrary tax'.

ELEVEN

A night to remember: Julia Cavendish and the *Titanic*

THERE CAN BE few disasters so well documented, or so deeply enshrined in the popular memory, as that of the sinking of the *Titanic* in the early hours of 15 April 1912. The largest passenger liner afloat struck an iceberg on its maiden transatlantic voyage, around 400 miles south of Newfoundland, and in less than three hours was lying on the seabed, a giant grave for almost 1,500 passengers and crew. Anyone who saw the film will recall the band playing on the sloping deck and remember distraught wives and children bundled into lifeboats leaving their men behind but still thinking it impossible that the *Titanic* would sink. In one of those boats was Mrs Julia Cavendish of Thurston near Bury St

Edmunds. She and her maid Nellie Barber clambered into lifeboat number six but her husband Tyrell stoically refused to leave the ship while there were women and children aboard. Like so many men crowding against the railings Tyrell could only watch as the lifeboat pulled away from the stricken liner and hope that Julia at least stood a chance of survival.

His prayers were answered. A Cunard liner picked up the lifeboat over an hour later, by which time the *Titanic* was on the sea-bed taking fifteen hundred lives with her. Julia was one of only 705 people to survive but she never saw her beloved husband again.

Tyrell and Julia had a whirlwind romance. He had met Chicago-born Julia in 1904 at a dance in London and it was love at first sight. Julia Florence Siegel, then only eighteen, was at finishing school, but two weeks after they met they became engaged to be married. Tyrell came from an illustrious and well-established family that included the Duke of Devonshire as a distant cousin. Among his Suffolk ancestors was Sir John Cavendish, Lord Chief Justice of England, whose son was involved in the murder of Wat Tyler during the Peasants' Revolt. In revenge, the villagers pursued Sir John to Lakenheath where he was on circuit in Suffolk enforcing the Statute of Labourers. They captured him and dragged him back to Bury St Edmunds, where they beheaded him in the market place before ransacking his house in Cavendish.

In Glemsford, the neighbouring village to Cavendish, lived George Cavendish. George prospered at the court of Henry VIII and his *Life of Cardinal Wolsey* still stands as one of the nation's greatest biographies. George's brother William was Henry VIII's district representative as Receiver of the Properties of the Monasteries at their dissolution and was one of the Suffolk men who surrounded the Ipswich-born Thomas Wolsey and shared with him the highs and lows of his adventurous career.

The Cavendishes eventually left Suffolk but, at the beginning of April 1912, Tyrell and Julia, together with Julia's maid, Nellie Barber, were living in a rented cottage in the tiny hamlet of Battlies Green, near Bury St Edmunds (where their son Henry was born in 1908; a second son, Geoffrey, was born in 1910). Tyrell was having a new wing added to Thurston House, in Thurston village where he had become one of the principal landowners. His return to Suffolk brought him back to his family's roots in the nearby village of Cavendish, where his forebears were once lords of the manor.

Tyrell and Julia could not have missed the announcement by the White Star Line when amid a blaze of publicity it advertised the maiden voyage of the newest, largest and most sumptuous Royal Mail steamer in the world, the *Titanic*. Julia jumped at the chance to introduce her husband and children to her family and of being with Tyrell for two whole weeks. On their return they were to take up residence in Thurston, and Tyrell would realise his intention to stand for Parliament as member for Bury St Edmunds.

Their travelling companions, drawn from the social elite, included members of New York's high society: Colonel John Jacob Astor, the richest man in the world (travelling with his nineteen-year-old pregnant wife); J. Bruce Ismay, co-owner of the White Star Line; and the millionaire, Benjamin Guggenheim. For first class passengers there were numerous bars and restaurants, plus a library, veranda and palm court, gymnasium, Turkish bath with Moorish décor, plunge bath and swimming pool. Some of the luxurious staterooms had four-poster beds and real coal fires. *Titanic* was the equivalent of an eleven-storey building and for those in first class there was everything that a top luxury hotel would offer. For Julia and Tyrell it was the opportunity of a lifetime – to visit America and be part of maritime history.

Bookings were made for all five of the Cavendish household, and preparations began for their departure. Julia, Nellie and the two children were to travel down to Southampton by train and Tyrell would meet them there. It was as a result of their giving up the cottage at Battlies Green, and using their Staffordshire address when booking, that the local newspapers later missed the Suffolk connection.

Misfortune struck when one of the children, Geoffrey, became ill. It was hurriedly decided that the boys should stay in England with relatives but that Tyrell, Julia and Nellie should still go. Julia did not want to disappoint her American relatives and thought that as the children were still so young there would be plenty of other opportunities in the future. Tyrell, Julia and Nellie travelled as first class passengers and occupied cabin C46. The night before they were due to sail Tyrell Cavendish had a premonition of another and much greater misfortune. So strong was his sense of impending danger that he made his will. He confided his fears to his wife but it all seemed so unlikely. The *Titanic* was unsinkable. She was, after all, the biggest and most luxurious ship of her day.

Thus, on 10 April the *Titanic* set sail, under the command of Captain Edward J. Smith, known as 'the millionaires' captain'. Four days into the voyage Tyrell was still plagued by a sense of foreboding. Julia tried to convince him that all was well. She tried to laugh it off, and reassured him that they would soon reach New York, proving that he had nothing to worry about. The rumour in the lounges and smoking rooms was that the chief engineer had been summoned by the White Star Line's managing director to discuss the possibility of a transatlantic speed record. It was literally 'full speed ahead'!

Shortly before midnight on the 14 April *Titanic*'s hull struck an iceberg. There had been several warning messages sent about icebergs the previous day and the crew were on iceberg watch. A mist out at sea made visibility difficult but Frederick Fleet, in *Titanic*'s look-out cage, high above the fo'c'sle deck, saw something that made him reach for the brass bell above the crow's nest. His message to the bridge was 'Iceberg right ahead!'

The watch heard *Titanic* plough into the ice. Some of it bobbed along in the water, then disappeared. Several on board heard a deep rumbling noise, which lasted for a few seconds whilst others heard a scraping or grinding coming from the ship's hull. The lifeboats were prepared for launching, although many on board thought it was no more than a cautious response to a minor incident. Most of the passengers were reluctant to consider abandoning the ship, besides which it was very cold on deck and the *Titanic* was surrounded by ice.

In number 6 boiler room the stoker knew differently. He had heard the impact and before his eyes a thin line of water began to pour through a crack in the hull.

Being first-class passengers Tyrell and Julia, with Nellie, had access to the decks and they all found places in the sixth lifeboat, under the command of quartermaster Robert Hichens. But Tyrell refused his place, saying there were still women and children aboard, and at 12.55 a.m. lifeboat six was launched. It had a capacity of sixty-five but initially set out only half full.

Many *Titanic* myths grew up and have flourished but few are more vivid than the story of Molly Brown. Chiefly because of the musical later written about the 'heroine' of lifeboat six, *The Unsinkable Molly Brown*, her story lives on. At Molly's insistence the lifeboat went back to rescue more people until Quartermaster Hichens insisted they had to be clear of the *Titanic*'s suction. Asked afterwards how she felt, Molly Brown answered 'Typical Brown luck', adding 'We're unsinkable'. And so the legend of what happened in lifeboat six began and Molly became, unlike the *Titanic*, unsinkable.

Might Julia have been able to see her husband once more, or was he lost in the chaotic crowds of men and women trying to stay upright against the angle of the deck, ever shifting as the stern lifted higher out of the water? Inside the furnishings and fittings were smashing and sliding towards the bow and one by one the porthole lights went out. And still the band played famously on, the sound carrying eerily across an otherwise silent sea, until the last hope was gone.

The 705 survivors, including those in lifeboat six, were rescued within hours by the Cunard liner *Carpathia*. Molly Brown had shared her thick clothing with some of the other women, and kept them warm by having them take turns at desperately rowing the lifeboat away from the ship's powerful suction. They would all have witnessed the final sinking of the *Titanic* at 2.20 a.m. on the morning of 15 April.

At six o'clock on the same morning, Julia and Nellie were among those taken on board the *Carpathia*. They were safe, though Julia never received her father's Marconigram message, written but not transmitted because the operators were too busy with official messages to trouble over individual ones. It read 'Anxious to know if both safe, your father Henry Siegel.' The Siegel family was frantic for news and Henry tried sending the message to the *Carpathia*, hoping his daughter and her husband would read it together. But it was not to be.

Tyrell's body was recovered by the Cable Ship *MacKay-Bennett*, one of four ships chartered by the White Star Line to search for bodies. It was one of the few identified and was eventually forwarded to Julia, together with his gold watch and a pair of gold cuff links.

Heartbroken, Julia returned to England and her children but could not face returning without Tyrell to the Suffolk home, so lovingly restored in the happy years of her marriage. She deposited his ashes in a wall safe at Golder's Green cemetery and the Thurston property was sold. Their two sons Henry and Geoffrey grew up in Staffordshire and Julia never remarried.

Julia never spoke about her loss, or about the *Titanic*, to her family. It was not only that she was maintaining both her dignity and privacy, but the cult of the *Titanic* was not then underway. After the initial headline-grabbing reporting of the *Titanic* Inquiry the furore died down, only to resurface in the 1950s when Walter Lord published his bestselling book, *A Night to Remember*, a historical documentary about the tragic events of 1912. The book was one of the first to combine hard, factual commentary with personal memories and was credited with launching the phenomenon of Titanomania.

Julia Cavendish died in 1963, over fifty years after the death of her husband. It was only in the early 1970s that the family discovered a secret that Julia had kept for all that time. Among the papers inherited by her son Geoffrey was a copy of Tyrell's will, and in it was mention of Thurston House. Intrigued by this undiscovered piece of family history Geoffrey, together with his daughter and son-in-law, decided to visit Suffolk to see where Julia and Tyrell had intended to live together. To his amazement and joy they discovered that, unknown to the family, Julia had paid for a village hall to be built in memory of her husband, named Cavendish Hall. Inside he found a photograph of his mother and a commemorative plaque to his father that reads:

> THIS HALL WAS BUILT AND GIVEN
> TO THE
> PEOPLE OF THURSTON
> BY
> JULIA F. CAVENDISH
> IN MEMORY OF HER HUSBAND
> TYRRELL WILLIAM CAVENDISH
> WHO LOST HIS LIFE ON THE S.S. 'TITANIC'
> APRIL 15, 1912.

This was the first the family knew of either Thurston House or Cavendish Hall. The spelling of Tyrell's name takes the older family form, used by his father Charles Tyrrell Cavendish, and was inherited from Mary, daughter of Sir Timothy Tyrrell of Shotover Park in Oxfordshire, who had married a Cavendish ancestor, Sir William, in 1676. Although the spelling on the plaque is often remarked on, Julia would undoubtedly have given the engraver precise instructions, though she probably never saw the finished plaque. For the rest of her life she kept secret the knowledge of her tribute to a husband with whom she had lived for such a short time but with whom she had been so happy. It might also have been in her mind to restore the Cavendish family name to Suffolk, in accordance with his wishes.

Geoffrey told his brother Henry about Thurston House and he, too, travelled to see the Hall. Henry continued his family's links with Suffolk by visiting Thurston on several occasions, becoming a pen-pal of the village schoolchildren who used Cavendish Hall. The children were fascinated by the family history and Henry would often call in on his way to attend reunions at his Cambridge college.

Among Julia's papers her sons also found their mother's account of the night of 14 April 1912, contained in two secret letters which were kept hidden until after her death. Henry's son, William Cavendish, writes: 'My grandmother's account of her experience when the *Titanic* sank are our only mementoes. We think she deliberately closed that episode of her life. My cousin has the watch my grandfather was wearing when he drowned.'

Julia's papers and the two letters remain private to the family.

TWELVE

Death in the skies

ON THE NIGHT of 16 June 1917 the Zeppelin L48 took off from Nordholz airship station just north of Bremerhaven in Germany, its mission to attack southern England and London in particular. At an altitude of 16,000 feet, the 644-foot-long airship cruised towards the Suffolk coast with its cargo of bombs and seventeen crew members in the gondolas slung below the huge cigar-shaped structure.

The L48 had made her maiden flight at Friedrichshafen on 22 May 1917 and was the last of Germany's assembly of military airships to be built. The very strong framework was made of aluminium and divided into compartments each of which contained a balloon inflated with hydrogen. Soon after the outbreak of the First World War Germany began using Zeppelins, developed by Ferdinand Zeppelin in 1900, for bombing raids and, because of its geographical position, East Anglia bore the brunt of the campaign. The ability of the airships to fly far above the altitude range of the anti-aircraft guns made them appear invincible.

They were lighter than air, could carry 4,400 lb (2,000 kg) of bombs, and were capable of travelling at speeds of up to 85 miles per hour. The L48 had on board a special passenger, Korvettenkapitan Victor Schutze, commodore of the North Sea Airship Division, who was in the rear gondola. In all probability it was Schutze who took her up to maximum altitude, eager to test the capabilities of Germany's new Zeppelin. The airships would need to go higher as British defences improved.

At around 1.30 a.m. on the morning of the 17 June it was clear that, for some reason, there was an engine malfunction. Aware that he had probably triggered it off by flying at such an ambitious height the commodore ordered a descent. But as the L48 came directly above the coastline the engines began gasping for oxygen. The compass froze and the crew experienced the first signs of frostbite while frantically trying to carry out repairs. Something had gone dramatically wrong.

The airship was first sighted forty miles north-east of Harwich and reported heading for Orfordness, from where Captain Robert Saundby (later Air Marshall Sir Robert) immediately sent up two aircraft, but they could fly no higher than 2,000 feet below the L48.

At 1.50 a.m. she began her enforced descent and on reduced power started to drift. The crew ditched their bombs in the vicinity of Martlesham Heath, but to no good effect. The Zeppelin veered round Wickham Market, past Woodbridge, and on towards Saxmundham.

By 3.15 a.m. anti-aircraft guns had her in their sights, and aircraft from Royal Flying Corps (RFC) Orfordness began their attack, flying at a then perilous altitude of 12,000 feet, immediately below the Zeppelin.

As the L48 descended further, a third plane, carrying eight double drums of ammunition, was despatched and began firing incendiary bullets. At the same time the ground artillery opened up.

For forty minutes the hurricane of fire continued, then those on the ground saw the Zeppelin come into view, twisting and turning, a perpendicular column of smoke rising higher and higher into the air. This 'aerial tornado' of horrific proportions left a trail of thick, black smoke that hung in the air for almost a quarter of an hour afterwards and was seen as far away as north Essex.

Unable to name the site for security reasons, a correspondent described the attack in the *East Anglian Daily Times*:

> Was it a dream, or was there a new disturbance in the air, not quite the noise of a train, but something like one travelling in the sky overhead? Before I could get my boots on guns at a distance began to roar. Pulling the bedroom blind on one side I saw the distant horizon lighted up as if by summer lightning with sparkling flashes of shellfire. The noise increased till it was evident that there was a terrific encounter between aircraft and land guns. The firing grew with intensity until there was a cannonade such as has never been heard on the coast since the days when Dutch and English fought at the Medway, or Sole Bay.

Ten minutes later the L48's heaving balloon of a body exploded. It weighed around twelve tons and contained around 400,000 cubic feet of hydrogen, which had ignited with horrendous consequences. A vast fireball, still erupting like an angry volcano, blazed its red light across the skies and took almost five minutes to nosedive to earth, a trail of smoke a mile long visible in the clear, early morning sky.

It has never been fully established just which aircraft fired the bullet that brought her down since the airship's 78-foot diameter kept the three planes out of sight of one another. It may have been a single bullet that punctured one of the hydrogen-filled gasbags, but whatever the cause the result was the same. Still on fire she crash-landed, stern first, at an angle of sixty degrees in a field near Holly Tree Farm, Theberton, her blazing structure shattering in the horrific inferno. Pieces of the falling airship were spread over a wide area and the darts of flaming metal spraying out from the descending fireball were seen as far away as Bungay. It was the first and last mission of Zeppelin L48.

Thinking they were over the sea off Harwich several of the crew including Kapitanleutnant Franz Eichler had jumped without parachutes. The others were incinerated on impact. Only three men emerged alive: Oberleutnant Mieth, the observation officer, and two other men who were helped to safely by PC Kiddle of the local constabulary.

The aftermath was strangely quiet. The morning of 17 June was glorious, the sky cloudless and, as one eye-witness said afterwards, 'as beautiful as only an early morning June sky can be'. The comparison with the earlier terrifying display of aerial pyrotechnics dropping out of nowhere onto the peaceful rural scene of Holly Tree Farm lent an air of eerie unreality.

Among the first officials to arrive on the scene were the civilian and naval draftsmen who faced the awesome task of detailing and investigating the incident and gaining what intelligence they could from the mangled wreckage. Naval engineers set up a marquee and such was the volume of sightseers and souvenir hunters that soldiers were drafted in to guard the wreck.

Within hours sightseers began to arrive in droves and by Sunday the numbers were said by the local paper to have exceeded thirty thousand. They came from neighbouring farms, on foot and on bicycle. From further afield, on hastily arranged excursions and by public transport, came souvenir hunters eager for a piece of the shattered metal. A collection was made for the Ipswich and East Suffolk Hospital that amounted to £30.

Visitors wanted to hear the story of the Zeppelin's dramatic and exciting demise and soon they were able to buy postcards to send to their friends, courtesy of a local photographer, John Smellie Waddell of the Hayling Studio in Leiston whose nephew was editor of the *Leiston Observer*. A series of postcards was produced and *A Pictorial Souvenir of the 'Strafed' Zeppelin L48* published and sold for one shilling.

The Southwold Press published a poem by W. S. Montgomery, a blind organ-grinder from Westleton, which sold for one penny and included the verse:

Quickly the crowds did gather to witness the dreadful scene
A mass of burning wreckage with the corpses in between,
Some of crew jumped from her, but that proved a certain death,
And those who stayed were burned alive, we gazed with shuddering breath.

An eye-witness told the press that her garden at Blythburgh had been littered with pieces of the Zeppelin's burnt-out fuselage, and another complained that after the crash the standing corn in nearby fields was trampled down by people taking short cuts to the scene from all directions.

One of the later-to-be Theberton churchwardens remembered being hoisted onto his father's shoulders at Walberswick to see the falling wreckage. His sister, a student at St Felix School in Southwold, cycled with friends the twenty-odd miles there and back on their day off to view the strafed airship and was offered singed buttons as keepsakes.

Almost every home in the area had a piece of the Zeppelin to display on the mantelpiece. Manufactured souvenirs were soon available and even included matchboxes, embroidered with an airship and two FE2B biplanes which had been instrumental in bringing down the Zeppelin. Parts of the aluminium structure were fashioned into ashtrays, bracelets, rings, aeroplanes and tiny replicas of the L48 herself. Despite the best efforts of the souvenir hunters, however, there were still huge piles of airship remains and debris to be loaded into trucks and taken to a nearby goods yard in Leiston. In addition to the unaccustomed activity on the ground, planes circled overhead capturing photographic evidence. Captain W. Walden Hammond, who formed the Photographic Flights Section of RFC Orfordness in 1916, made several trips over the burnt-out skeleton of the L48.

A piece of the framework still survives in Theberton church and another, fashioned into an ashtray stand, is at the old Garrett engineering works, now the Long Shop Museum, in Leiston. When war broke out staff at Garretts had been in a difficult position. In the 1880s John and Henry Garrett had gone to Germany to set up an operation in Magdeburg which for many years did business with the Leiston works. On hearing that no one would dig graves for the German crew of the L48, Frank Garrett allowed the women in the munitions department to volunteer for the task.

Arrangements were made for the immediate burial of the sixteen Germans who had perished in the crash, their coffins made by Cutts of Leiston, contractors to the War Office. The rector, a brigade chaplain and a Catholic priest officiated; the bodies were borne on gun carriages and army wagons. They were laid to rest in Theberton cemetery where they remained for fifty years, close to the magnificent fourteenth-century, thatched Church of St Peter, with its round Norman tower, set in the very essence of the Suffolk countryside. For the duration of the war, and for some years afterwards, there was some ill feeling about the graves, but it gradually faded and they were tended as carefully as any others in the churchyard. The stones, one for each of the sixteen men, were set flat within a stone border memorial, sent there from Germany: first by sea to Southampton, then by train to Leiston and finally to Theberton by horse and cart. The inscription read: 'Who art thou that judgest another man's servant? To his own master he standeth or falleth.'

In 1967 Kapitanleutnant Eichler and his crew were reinterred with three other Zeppelin crews at the German war cemetery at Cannock Chase in Staffordshire. A plaque in Theberton cemetery now marks the place where they were buried.

The effects of the Zeppelin bombing campaign on the civilian population cannot be overstated. Until the beginning of the twentieth century Britain's main defence force was the Navy, since potential invaders had of necessity to arrive in boats and advance inland on foot. The First World War was the first time that bombs reached the civilian population from the air and this engendered an unfamiliar sense of vulnerability. Defence against aerial attack was something new and aircraft capabilities relatively undeveloped. No wonder a reporter on the local newspaper wrote on the 17 June: 'Suddenly, whilst apparently a long way up in a north-easterly direction, the Zeppelin was seen to break into a ball of flames. The cheers that rose from thousands of throats showed plainly the relief that was experienced that another night prowler had found a fast fate.'

After the destruction of the L48 there were far fewer Zeppelin raids. The designers of the L48 were devastated by her failure and shocked at the loss of Commodore Schutze. British aerial and gun defences greatly improved during 1917 while ground-based searchlights were developed. Nearly 6,000 bombs were dropped on the British mainland by the Zeppelins, killing 556 civilians and military personnel, and a further 1,358 were injured in the attacks.

THIRTEEN

Genius: Benjamin Britten and the story of Snape

SNAPE, WITH ITS intensely beautiful river setting and its multifarious artistic and industrial connections, draws together in one small place an essence of the county of Suffolk that is unique. 'If music be the food of love,' wrote Shakespeare, 'play on; give me excess of it, that, surfeiting, the appetite may sicken, and so die.' At Snape Maltings, since 1967 a venue for internationally renowned music, and the home of the famous Aldeburgh Festival, there is no such thing as an excess of music.

The tiny port of Snape claims a tradition of seagoing trade since the Viking longboats navigated their way up the river Alde, but the warehouses and maltings complex seen today were built by Newson Garrett. Newson was born in Leiston in 1812, the son of Richard Garrett, whose family was both enterprising and ambitious. One branch worked the smithy at Wickham Market where it held sway for several hundred years. A Garrett ancestor cast the bells for the church in Wickham Market but in 1636 emigrated to New England with a group of Puritans, although America was not to his taste and twenty years later he returned home to Suffolk.

Richard's branch of the Garrett family made edge-tools in Woodbridge, their scythes and sickles of such a high standard that the Garrett trademark was sometimes forged. In 1778 Richard Garrett married Elizabeth Newson, the heiress to an agricultural machinery business at Leiston, and so began the engineering dynasty of Richard Garrett and Sons. The firm would eventually employ 2,500 men and women and sustain that part of Suffolk throughout the nineteenth and early twentieth centuries, their progressive engineering development becoming world-renowned. For the Great Exhibition of 1851, in the Crystal Palace, Richard Garrett and Sons mounted a large display of portable steam engines. In honour of the occasion 300 workmen and their wives were taken to London from Slaughden Quay on two of the Garretts' schooners. They landed at Horseferry Wharf and walked to the exhibition halls in Hyde Park.

Richard's three sons were brought up in the expansive and prosperous days of the early part of the Industrial Revolution, but as the youngest son Newson would not inherit the Leiston works. He therefore set out to make his own way in life and went to London where he met and married Louisa Dunnell in 1834. When Richard Garrett died in 1837 Newson and Louisa decided to return to Suffolk with their children and, in 1841, bought the business of Osborne and Fennell, corn and coal merchants at Snape Bridge. Newson Garrett and his family were to make an indelible mark on the commercial and political scene at Snape and nearby Aldeburgh and two of his daughters may rightly claim international fame.

Elizabeth Garrett Anderson (1836–1917), Newson's second daughter, was one of the country's first women doctors and, as mayor of Aldeburgh in 1908, the first woman mayor in England. Against initial opposition from her father, and wholly against the Victorian ethos of a woman's place being in the home, she entered the Middlesex Hospital as a medical student in 1860. Eventually, with the help of her husband, James Skelton Anderson, she succeeded in setting up her own dispensary for women and children in Marylebone and in 1872 the Elizabeth Garrett Anderson Hospital for Women opened its doors. Together with a younger sister, Millicent, she also became a well-known advocate for women's suffrage. Millicent, later Dame Millicent Garrett Fawcett, was born in Aldeburgh in 1847. She married Henry Fawcett, the blind Postmaster-General, and with his help set about trying to gain the vote for women. She was for many years the president of the National Union for Women's Suffrage Societies and launched the lectures that led to the founding of Newnham College, Cambridge. According to a writer in the *Suffolk Mercury*, Elizabeth and Millicent 'almost alone, have raised the whole platform [of feminism] to the level of respectability'.

In the same year that Elizabeth was elected mayor of Aldeburgh, Emmeline Pankhurst and her daughter Christabel were jailed for their part in the demonstrations for the right to vote. But Millie, as her family and friends knew her, continued to lead her NUWSS peacefully. She believed in 'quiet persuasion and argument'.

Within three years of Newson Garrett's arrival in Snape, 17,000 quarters of barley were being shipped annually from the premises to nearby breweries and to London. His daughter Millicent described her father as 'ambitious, impulsive, impatient and quarrelsome' but it was this side of his inquisitive, progressive nature that led to the rapid expansion of Snape Maltings. Soon he decided that instead of shipping the barley away he would turn the grain into malt and ship that to the breweries instead. Special malt houses were built and maltsters employed to work the kilns, which were housed in the new, mellow red-brick buildings with steep timber roofs and timber floors. The bricks were made at the Garrett brickworks in Snape and the roofs were originally finished with Welsh and Italian slates.

In 1859 Newson Garrett was responsible for the opening of a branch line of the Great Eastern Railway that ran from Snape to Saxmundham. By the time he died, in 1893, Newson had a busy and successful maltings, had built numerous ships and increased the amount of barge traffic up and down the river Alde, and had served the people and borough of Aldeburgh well. As late as 1964 there was still a descendant of Newson Garrett working as manager of the Maltings, although by then operational control had passed out of the family.

The Garrett barges continued to be regular visitors to the Snape quay until 1939 when war put a stop to the barge trade. In the 1960s the route was reopened but by then it was a motor barge, the *Atrato*, that brought bulk barley upriver from Lowestoft for the new owners, Gooderham and Hayward Limited.

In 1939 a young musician named Benjamin Britten, son of a Lowestoft dentist, decided to go to America. He went as a conscientious objector and was following in the footsteps of W. H. Auden whom he had met while composing music for documentary films put out by the General Post Office. While there he read an article by E. M. Forster entitled 'George Crabbe: The Poet and the Man'. It began:

> To talk about Crabbe is to talk about England. He never left our shores and he only once ventured to cross the border into Scotland. He did not even go to London much, but lived in villages and small country towns. He was a clergyman of the English Church. His Christian name was George, the name of our national saint. More than that, his father was called George, and so was his grandfather, and he christened his eldest son George, and his grandson was called George also. Five generations of George Crabbes!

The poet came from the same part of the world as Benjamin Britten – Suffolk. Crabbe was born in Aldeburgh in 1754 and Britten at Lowestoft in 1913, but there was an indissoluble link between them stretching across the years and across continents. Forster wrote of Suffolk, and its coast, and quoted from Crabbe's *The Borough*, which included the story of 'Peter Grimes', the savage fisherman who was accused of murdering his apprentices, a man so feared that no one would go fishing with him in his boat. Forster wrote evocatively of Aldeburgh, the sea, the Alde estuary, the flat Suffolk coast and the odour of brine and dirt tempered with the scent of flowers. Britten read the words and was reminded of Suffolk and of Crabbe's Aldeburgh. He said later that he was profoundly homesick: 'I felt a feeling of nostalgia for Suffolk where I had always lived . . . I suddenly realised where I belonged and what I lacked . . . I had become without roots.' He returned to Suffolk in 1942 and lived at The Old Mill, Snape, a converted windmill on the brow of a hill.

About five years later Britten and Eric Crozier were among a group of musicians travelling across Europe with the English Opera Group. They were on their way to a music festival at Lucerne in a programme that would include many international artists and British musicians who would stage Britten's *Albert Herring* and *The Rape of Lucretia*. Eric Crozier later wrote: 'We were proud to be presenting – for the first time – a group of forty British artists in such distinguished company; proud of the warm and appreciative response our new operas could draw from European audiences, proud that England was at last making some contribution to the traditions of international opera.'

It seemed absurd to be travelling across Europe to present British operas that no one at home would host. Why not have a music festival at home, in England, and where better than at Aldeburgh? The town had a long-established tradition of music, and an unbroken affinity with artists of all kinds. If such a festival was to succeed it could have no better home.

In 1947 Eric Crozier and Benjamin Britten hurried back to Suffolk and Aldeburgh. Frantic discussions took place and tea parties were given for local friends and acquaintances, all the time sounding out opinion. Problems there were bound to be, but there was at least a stage at Jubilee Hall, built by Newson Garrett as a gift to the town to commemorate Queen Victoria's Jubilee. A committee was appointed under the chairmanship of the Countess of Cranbrook and the Aldeburgh Festival was born. Due to space restrictions it would not be possible to stage lavish productions and some of the concerts would take place in the parish church. In January the following year a great many people packed into a public meeting to hear about the new festival. By the end of the evening, nearly £200 had been subscribed and enquiries began coming in for tickets and programmes before any were even available. Within a week a quarter of all tickets had been sold and a general offer of support was forthcoming from the Arts Council.

The first Aldeburgh Festival took place in 1948. Five operas, ten concerts and various lectures were performed over nine days. Over the next ten years the festival established itself as an annual event in the arts calendar as more and more visitors made the journey to this eastern part of Suffolk. The Jubilee Hall was by no means the ideal venue from the practical aspect, but it did have atmosphere and was beginning to take on a life of its own. What it was not, however, was profitable. Beset by financial worries, it was soon clear that the Aldeburgh Festival would have to be rethought and in 1954 the Festival Committee announced plans for the building of a new theatre in the belief that it would solve the perennial lack of money. But it was postponed and some of the concerts were moved to Blythburgh church instead. In 1960 the Jubilee Hall was enlarged sufficiently to begin attracting musicians of a high calibre. In 1961 Rostropovich gave his first concert at Aldeburgh and was the first of many international stars to attend.

By 1965 the festival had seriously outgrown its first home. It was neither practically nor financially feasible to build a new concert hall in Aldeburgh but a possible solution presented itself, just a few miles down the road at Snape.

As the twentieth century progressed new, mechanised methods of malting superseded those that in Newson Garrett's day had been so revolutionary. The seasonal nature of the work meant that men were employed only on maintenance for half of the year and in 1964 the last Snape maltsters went into voluntary liquidation, bringing to an end 120 years of the malting trade. For some time the vast complex of buildings stood empty until it was bought by an animal feed company, George Gooderham Investments. Gooderham and Hayward had manufactured feed at Marlesford since the nineteenth century and needed more space for milling and storage. They did not, however, require all the buildings and it was agreed that the Aldeburgh Festival would lease the largest of the malt houses in that part of the old Garrett complex that overlooked the marshes. Work began almost immediately to convert it into a concert hall.

The Snape Maltings Concert Hall was opened on 2 June 1967 by the Queen at the start of that year's festival. Conversion work had cost £175,000 and it was generally agreed to be among the finest small halls in the world. Almost overnight it became a vehicle for the artistic mind and heart of all who played or sang there, and it captured the loyalty of its audience not only because of the music but also because of its situation.

The view across the Alde estuary is unrivalled and timeless. The river margins are lined with reed beds and host, among other wildlife, one of the largest colonies of avocet in the country. Snape is only five miles from the sea, but nearer twenty by boat as the river twists and bends. At Snape Bridge the Alde becomes tidal and at high tide the water spreads out over the surrounding marshlands. The tiny church of St Botolph is visible just upriver, at Iken, built on the highest point of a bluff known as the Long Reach that juts out into the estuary. At low tide from a southwesterly approach the shape of the former island is still seen and is a marker for the boats and barges that have travelled the waterway for centuries.

The spirits of countless writers, poets and artists – J. M. Barrie, H. G. Wells, Thomas Carlyle, Edward FitzGerald, not forgetting George Crabbe and his ilk – all inhabit the collective memory of Snape and Aldeburgh. In 1860 Wilkie Collins went by the newly opened railway line to Aldeburgh and set his novel *No Name* in Aldeburgh. Edward Clodd, the rationalist, lived at Strafford House on Crag Path and held Whitsuntide gatherings which included visitors like H. G. Wells and Thomas Hardy.

Newson Garrett was a proclaimed patron of the arts and education. It is thanks to him that the Jubilee Hall was built, at his own expense, and he entertained friends who brought music to the social life of Aldeburgh in what was a quite prophetic way. The Garrett daughters would sing to the piano accompaniment of Mrs Percy Metcalf, whose husband introduced the music of Bach, Mozart and Handel. Millicent Garrett later remembered: 'I can hear now my sister Agnes singing Spohr's 'Who calls the Hunter to the Wood?' with the piano accompaniment in Mrs Metcalf's rather inadequate hands – and Mr M. playing the horn obligato.'

These recitals would be attended by among others Mrs James, the widowed grandmother of the antiquarian and writer M. R. James who lived in 'reduced circumstances' at Wyndham House in Aldeburgh. She enjoyed the music in the Garrett home, saying it reminded her of more prosperous days when she used to attend the opera. Montague 'M. R.' James, too, went there and employed a 'Mr Garrett' as the hero in *The Tractate Middoth*. (James's father was a curate at Aldeburgh in 1848, later becoming rector of Great Livermere near Bury St Edmunds.) In 1930 he wrote: 'Aldeburgh, "sung" by Crabbe and figuring in Wilkie Collins's *No Name*, has a special charm for those who, like myself, have known it from childhood; but I do not find it easy to put that charm into words.'

In the year that Newson Garrett died a pupil in one of the schools he had so enthusiastically encouraged was Theodore Francis Powys, a member of the famous Powys family of writers and artists. He attended Eaton House School in Aldeburgh and began his career at Sweffling, a few miles inland.

To these luminaries was now added the names of Benjamin Britten, Peter Pears, Imogen Holst, Eric Crozier and his wife, the mezzo-soprano Nancy Evans, E. M. Forster, Yehudi Menuhin, Dmitri Shostakovich, Mstislav Rostropovich, Janet Baker, Dietrich Fischer-Dieskau, Julian Bream, Oliver Messel, Joan Greenwood and composers Tippett, Copland, Poulenc . . . among others.

In 1969 disaster struck. During rehearsals of Mozart's *Idomeneo*, with Britten conducting, fire broke out and destroyed the concert hall. The opera was eventually staged in Blythburgh church and Britten vowed that, like the phoenix, Snape would rise again. It did. The Queen was able to reopen the Maltings Concert Hall in time for the start of the 1970 festival.

In 1965 Britten became a member of the Order of Merit. This was his most cherished honour. Only twenty-four people are allowed to be members at one time and since its creation in 1902 only two composers prior to Britten had received the honour. In June 1976 his lifetime contribution to music was acknowledged when he was awarded a life peerage. Although Britten had lived and worked in Aldeburgh since 1947 (first at Crag House and then

The Red House), in 1971 he and the singer Peter Pears bought Chapel House in Horham. They had so many visitors at The Red House in Aldeburgh, some invited and some not, that it became impossible for them to work.

Chapel House was bought as a retreat and although an extension was built to provide Britten with a large music room, it was a small studio that was built at the far end of the garden that was to become a 'composition hut'. There he is reputed to have composed some of his best-known works, including *Death in Venice*, *Phaedra* and his third string quartet. The tiny brick hut was built with no windows facing the house, a single doorway on the garden façade and a large window overlooking the fields, to limit the amount of domestic distraction. In 2002 the hut was declared a Grade II listed building, by Culture Secretary Tessa Jowell. She said: 'Benjamin Britten is without a doubt the greatest English classical composer of the last century. Britten's music studio, with its view across his beloved Suffolk countryside, is no architectural gem, but its importance as a piece of our cultural heritage cannot be denied.'

Britten died at Aldeburgh in December 1976 having been ill for some time. He was laid to rest in Aldeburgh churchyard, his grave lined with rushes gathered from Snape marshes by Bob and Doris Ling, who were the Concert Hall managers and long-standing friends. He left a legacy that has made a corner of Suffolk world-famous and created a centre for the renaissance of English composition.

The old barley store was converted into what is now the Britten-Pears School for Advanced Musical Studies and the entire maltings complex taken over by the Aldeburgh Foundation. Eminent musicians now attend the School, the Aldeburgh Festival has flourished and the Concert Hall is used throughout the year and for classical, folk and jazz concerts, opera, contemporary dance, lectures and a new innovation, the Aldeburgh Poetry Festival.

On the approach to Snape, along the Aldeburgh to Woodbridge road and over Snape Bridge, one of the first things to come into view is the topmast of the *Cygnet*, a barge built on the

Medway in 1881 and now moored at the quay. She is a Thames Spritsail barge, called a 'spritty' by the bargemen, and was used to carry small farm freights on the rivers to Ipswich, Felixstowe and Mistley and is a reminder of those times. Then the maltings become visible and the view from the Concert Hall is out over the magical, ethereal vista of the reed-lined Alde estuary. It leaves an indelible impression: you know you are somewhere special.

FOURTEEN

Sir Alf

THERE ARE TWO dates, it is said, that are etched forever on the minds of those who lived through them. What were you doing on the day that President Kennedy was assassinated, and what kind of day did you have on 30 July 1966? English football fans, and many others besides, will have no trouble in identifying the day when before a capacity attendance of 96,924 England beat Germany 4–2 in extra time to win the World Cup. What was special for Ipswich Town Football Club was that the hero of the hour was England manager, Alf Ramsey (1920–99) who had gone from Ipswich in 1963, after an eight-year reign at Portman Road, to be the full-time manager of England. There was intense countywide interest in the 1966 World Cup when, as coach, Ramsey steered the national team to triumph. He became the only England manager, before or since, to score a World Cup final victory. Those who could get near a television set on the day saw the victorious Bobby Moore lift high the Jules Rimet cup and 'the General' break into an uncharacteristic grin. Many brides who had chosen 30 July for their wedding smiled ruefully as their male guests sneaked out to the car park to tune in to the car radio. Alf Ramsey is not just a football hero but he's a Suffolk legend, too, and is close to the hearts of 'Blues' supporters young and old alike.

Alfred Ernest Ramsey was born 'over the border' at Dagenham in Essex in 1920, some nine years before Henry Ford turned the first sod on an area of 500 acres which was to make Dagenham and the Ford Works synonymous. Alf was one of four sons of Albert and Florence Ramsey, born on 22 January. Their father ran a smallholding and, while the Ramsey boys thrived in a still rural Dagenham, their family circle was close and defensive. The Ramseys suffered local abuse as they were thought to be gypsies; indeed Alf was often cruelly called 'darkie'. But such treatment taught the youngster to disguise his emotions and to adopt a stoic approach to adversity, assets that would in the future serve him well.

Later he 'improved' his Essex accent by listening and copying BBC newsreaders and developed the habit of saying as little as possible, a habit that was to bring him into conflict with members of the press towards the end of his career as English manager.

Alf and his brothers walked around four miles to their school at Becontree Heath. It kept them fit and the boys would play on a meadow at the back of the house and bounce a ball back and forth between them on their walks to school. In *Talking Football* Alf recalled:

> I lived for the open air from the moment I could toddle. The meadow at the back of our cottage was our playground. For hours every day, with my brothers, I learnt how to kick, head, and control a ball, starting first of all with a tennis ball, and it is true to say that we found all our pleasure that way. We were happy in the country, the town and cinemas offering no attractions for us, and it was not until I had reached the age of fourteen that I first saw a film.

Aged seven Alf was picked to play for the school football team, at inside-left, buying his first pair of football boots for just under five shillings (twenty-five pence). His mother gave him four shillings and he saved up the eleven pence himself, an early sign of self-reliance. Like many youngsters of the moneybox era he extracted the pennies with the help of a kitchen knife, proud that he could contribute a little. He wrote that if the boots had been made of gold and studded with diamonds he would not have felt prouder than when he first put them on and strutted around the dining room, only to be reprimanded by his mother fearful for her lino!

When he was nine, in the same year that Fords began to transform Dagenham from a country backwater into part of London's concrete jungle, Alf was made captain of the school team. He left school in 1934 and, not surprisingly, followed his classmates in applying for a job at Fords, which he failed to get. Instead he decided to become a grocer, a practical option in the fast-expanding Dagenham, and managed to get an apprenticeship at the local Co-op as a delivery boy. He cycled round the housing developments delivering groceries. This helped his fitness and enabled him to boost his mother's housekeeping. The downside was that he could not play football since he had to work on Saturdays.

At about this time the manager of a nearby sweet shop, Edward Grimme, saw the need to get several of the local lads together for a Thursday afternoon's football, Thursday being their half day. The Five Elms United team was formed, and before long Alf joined. He enjoyed being back on the football pitch, although the Five Elms consisted mainly of apprentices and school-leavers who had to play against older men. But he considered this good training and said later that he had learned several valuable lessons in those days.

In 1937 Five Elms FC came under the scrutiny of a scout from Portsmouth, Ned Liddle, who showed interest in the young centre-half, Alf Ramsey. They offered him a trial as an amateur, with a view towards his eventually turning professional. His family was not at all sure what to make of the possibility of Alf becoming a footballer although his father made no attempt to dissuade him. It seemed a safer bet to stay on at the Co-op and hope for a better, steady job. No one in the Ramsey circle had ever entertained such ambitions, nor indeed had Alf himself. He was not a boy who spent much time day-dreaming and if he had it would be of having his own greengrocery, not playing football for Portsmouth. The country was just emerging from the depths of the Depression and getting a good job was a top priority for working-class England. Amateur status would mean he could hang on to his job at the Co-op in case, as he fully expected, he found himself back at Dagenham. He had no confidence that he could, or would, make football his career.

After much deliberation Alf signed a contract with Portsmouth but heard nothing. He was glad, then, that he had not been carried away by unattainable dreams, and slipped back into his job at the Oxlow Lane Co-op and kicking a ball about on the meadow behind the Merry Fiddlers pub.

At the outbreak of war football took a back seat in the nation's concerns and in June 1940 Alf was called up and sent to Truro in Cornwall. It was the furthest he had been from home but he quickly adapted to the new surroundings and company. Before long he helped form a battalion team. Sergeant Ramsey was back on a football pitch. In 1943 his army team was invited to the Dell to play Southampton, Alf as captain. Surprisingly they were only beaten 10–3, Southampton scoring five goals in each half. Far from being disheartened, Alf was buoyed up by having played faster and better opposition and was pleased when the team was asked back to the Dell to play the reserve side. This time the battalion team won 4–1 for, as captain, Alf was beginning to put into practice his footballing intelligence. It was not enough to kick the ball in the right direction, there had to be strategy. One or two on the Southampton touchline were impressed with Alf's performance and he was asked to join their first team.

Memories of his Portsmouth experience, coupled with a deep-seated modesty and lack of confidence, made him hesitate. Was he good enough to play professional football? Did he even want to?

Alf's commanding officer took a more positive view and arranged for him to meet the Southampton team. Possibilities began to open up before him, but he still wondered if he could do it, although by this time he was beginning to develop a little ambition. One thing troubled him, though, and that was his age.

Twenty-two was fairly old to be making his debut so he began to tell people he had been born in 1922, not 1920. This juggling with dates was to continue and in his autobiography, *Talking Football*, he wrote that he was born in 1922 and was only twenty-two when he made his senior debut, when in fact he was twenty-four. At about the same time he perfected the inscrutable, detached demeanour that was to become his trademark and earn him the nickname 'Old Stoneface'.

With the end of the war in sight Alf signed for Southampton, the manager agreeing that if it did not work out he could leave at the end of the 1944/45 season. He still had it in the back of his mind that if he failed he could return to his old job at the Dagenham Co-op. But he was good enough for Southampton to invite him back for a second season. This boosted his confidence and when he was demobbed in June 1946 the new Southampton manager made him a permanent offer. However, as a young man seeking security in an insecure world, Alf turned it down. He was twenty-six and knew that a career in professional football at his age would last little longer than five years. But Southampton upped their offer and Alf Ramsey became a professional footballer.

Alf's career took off. In 1949 he left Southampton for Tottenham Hotspur for £21,000, a record transfer fee for a full back at the time. Starting at Southampton as an inside right, he had moved to centre half and then into defence in the right-back position, where he stayed. His interest lay not just in running with the ball but in tactics and at White Hart Lane his natural leadership on the pitch earned him the nickname 'the General'. Having been exiled from Essex for some years he now returned to his parents' home in Dagenham. Tottenham won the Second Division championship in 1950 and the First Division championship the following year.

The 1949/50 season saw England competing in the World Cup for the first time. The competition, founded in 1930 by Frenchman Jules Rimet, was held in Brazil. Alf Ramsey was in the team, though it went badly. The players were ill- prepared for the conditions they met there. They arrived jet-lagged and with no previous opportunities, in a pre-television era, of seeing how South American teams played. When they did, England was awe-struck. Alf wrote: 'During our training spells two things quickly impressed themselves upon me. The first was that during practice matches I found it very hard to breathe. Secondly, at the conclusion of even an easy kick about, I felt infinitely more tired than after a hectic league match at home.'

In November 1950 Alf was asked to captain England. Billy Wright was injured and Alf took his place. Among the many telegrams of congratulations, including one from Billy Wright, was one from Alf's fiancée, Victoria (Vickie) Answorth, whom he married in 1951. During his playing career he represented England thirty-one times.

The end of Alf Ramsey's playing career came in the 1954/55 season. Alf was thirty-four and had suffered several nagging injuries, besides which a promising young player named Danny Blanchflower had arrived at White Hart Lane. Alf decided it was time to hang up the boots and move on. In August 1955 he met with the directors of Ipswich Town Football Club who offered him the manager's job. Spurs agreed to release him and Alf surprised everyone by taking on a small-town team languishing in the old Third Division.

Although the Ipswich Association Football Club had been formed in 1878 it was 1936 before the club turned professional. On Saturday 29 August of that year the team turned out in the new royal-blue-and-white strip and, wrote Tony Garnett of the *East Anglian Daily Times*:

> Everybody involved in bringing professional football to Ipswich attended a pre-match luncheon at the Great White Horse, the most fashionable hotel in town in those days. A toast was proposed by Stanley Rous (later to become Sir Stanley) who was secretary of the Football Association and a Suffolk man. Captain 'Ivan' Cobbold, the Town chairman, responded. The band of the Scots Guards (Cobbold's regiment) paraded and Ipswich Town Football Club was launched with due ceremony.

A crowd of 14,211 turned out on a sweltering hot day, many of them farmers who had yet to complete the harvest. The 'Town' beat Tunbridge Wells Rangers 4–1, George Dobson scoring Ipswich's first professional goal at the Portman Road ground, which took its name from the ancient office of Portmen in the borough of Ipswich, and had been used as a football pitch as early as 1884. (Prior to that they had played at Brooks Hall, off the Norwich Road, and as there were no changing rooms the team used the Inkerman pub across the road.)

By the time Alf arrived at Portman Road in 1955 the Town was enjoying its football and had, apparently, no real ambition to advance further into the big time. They won the Southern League championship at their first attempt and in 1938/39 gained entry into league football. After a brief exposure to the Second Division for the 1953/54 season, Ipswich slipped back into the Third Division the following year. Alf Ramsey was about to change all that.

The atmosphere at Portman Road was one that Alf could relate to. Although a town, Ipswich had the feel of a rural backwater and the club was a friendly place. It was run and funded by the ubiquitous Cobbold family whose money came from the brewing industry. Backwater it might have been but there was not the degree of class tension attached to it of the sort that was to dog relations between Alf and the FA later in his career. However, possibly intimidated by 'moving up in the world', from the pitch to the boardroom, Alf thought he should improve his speaking voice and to this end took elocution lessons. This was later cruelly satirised and gave rise to false accusations of a betrayal of his humble origins. Such unfair and misplaced accusations merely confirmed to Alf that life was neither fair nor easy and the stoicism built up during his teenage years saw him in good stead.

His time at Ipswich, though, was progressive and productive. He said later that he had no set plan when he came to Ipswich, especially as he had been used to First Division play. What he found at Portman Road was a long way from that, but what he did find was a team with plenty of potential and an open-minded, friendly club atmosphere. His first game as manager was against Torquay, which they lost 2–0. The local press said it was 'as poor a performance as one can recollect at Portman Road'. Alf had little to lose and everything to gain.

To boost the team Alf turned to Portsmouth, where he had so nearly gone as a player at the start of his career, and in 1958 signed Ray Crawford for £5,000. A good move, as it turned out, as Crawford went on to score twenty-five goals in thirty matches for Ipswich. Encouraged, Alf began to raise the stakes. He signed Andy Nelson from West Ham for £8,500 and, with Ted Phillips opting to stay at Ipswich, the team began to copy the new tactics and formations being tried out by the First Division. The players acquired a nickname – 'Ramsey's Rustics' – a sure sign that Ipswich was being noticed.

Ipswich was promoted to the First Division in 1961 and a second triumph followed almost immediately. Alf's faith in the team, and his own calculated ambition and skill, had taken the 'Rustics' a long way past their supporters' hopes or expectations. For his part, Alf was back where he had left off – this time managing rather than playing First Division football. Under a regime of mutual respect between manager and players 'plucky little Ipswich', as they were patronisingly called by the national press, showed dogged determination in clocking up points as the season progressed. It was still a pre-television age and, just as England had been unable to study the opposition in the World Cup, so the league teams were more and more unsure about what they would face on the pitch. The days when everyone went out and played the same game, either better or worse, were over. The hand on the tiller was becoming increasingly important and Alf Ramsey was one of the first to begin stamping his own methods on the game.

Half-way through the season the press began to smell a possibility of success as the 'Rustics' piled on the points. Attention was drawn not just to the team but to its manager; press coverage began to include studies of 'Mr Alfred Ramsey'. In the last game of the season Ipswich were at home to Aston Villa in front of almost thirty thousand supporters. If they won they would have fifty-six points and be crowned champions. Ray Crawford came through with two goals and the tension mounted. There was no punching the air or arm waving from the bench. Mr Alfred Ramsey sat stony-faced, but intent on the game, as news came through that Burnley, the other contender for the title, had been held to a draw by Chelsea. 'Ramsey's Rustics' had done it! They were First Division champions in their first season and all Suffolk celebrated. Alf and the chairman of the club, John Cobbold, even did a lap of honour.

The following season the strain began to show and it looked as though the Ramsey magic had evaporated. There were injuries to key players and Ipswich appeared to have gone too far too fast with limited resources. Alf couldn't buy the replacements he needed and the team struggled. The element of surprise that had been successful lost its sting as other sides were coming up with their own surprise tactics. Money was an ongoing problem for, as nearly all the club's revenue came in at the gates, they needed to keep winning.

These were exciting, if troubled, times at Portman Road but it was no less so with the national side. England manager Walter Winterbottom stood down after a disappointing performance in the 1962 World Cup and the FA turned its attention to the headline-grabbing Ipswich and its increasingly high-profile manager. In October they sounded out Alf Ramsey with a view to offering him the England manager's job. But would he leave Ipswich? He had a close relationship with the club at all levels and it would be a wrench to leave, especially when he was most needed. To be invited to take the England job, however, was an irresistible challenge for any manager. Alf agreed and, on 25 October 1962, shortly after Ipswich's roller-coaster participation in the European Cup, he was appointed England manager, effective from 1 May 1963. Jackie Milburn stepped in to take over at Portman Road. Alf had been at Ipswich eight years and in that time had transformed not just his club but also the way English football was played. He left Ipswich Town at the end of April although he continued to live in the town and travel where he had to by train. Sitting alone, and often unrecognised, he later said that many of his important decisions were made while rattling through the East Anglian countryside. 'I can't read on trains,' he said, 'but I can think.'

The three year lead-up to the now legendary story of England's only World Cup success took place in the shadow of Alf Ramsey's outright prediction that England would win, made on his first day in the job. It seemed to be more of a promise than a prediction but focused attention on the team's preparations and personalities. The heat was on and it remained to be seen if he could do for England what he had done for Ipswich.

It was during the preparations for the World Cup that Ramsey's 'wingless wonders' began to feature in the pundits' pages. This groundbreaking strategy of lining up players behind the strikers, leaving no recognised players on the flanks, was a bold tactic. Wingers had been part of the English game since long before anyone could remember and the 'wingless wonders' idea would need a lot of proving.

Ramsey's first England match saw the national team defeated 5–2 by France in what is now known as the European Championships. But there were still three years to go before the World Cup and plenty of time for Ramsey to mould a team that would be capable of fulfilling his prophecy.

Around this time a definite rift began to open up between the man of humble but solid beginnings and his masters at the FA. He referred to the men in suits as 'those people', and while many might have agreed with him, 'those people' were the ones with the power and influence. But for the moment Alf Ramsey had the floor. His triumph against West Germany at Wembley in July 1966 put a smile on the face of English football. The magical, if controversial, scoreline of 4–2 is enshrined in the nation's history. Kenneth Wolstenholme's now famous commentary of the final minutes in the match has been quoted endlessly and evokes a wistful nostalgia for a bygone year when an English captain wiped his hands clean of the Wembley mud to shake the Queen's gloved hand. Who can forget the words: 'Some people are on the pitch. They think it's all over . . .' and, as Geoff Hurst slammed in England's fourth goal, the roar of the home crowd almost drowned out the referee's final whistle and Wolstenholme's '. . . it is now!'

Alf Ramsey had reached the pinnacle of his career, and what an achievement it was. The toothless grin of Nobby Stiles, dancing on the pitch with the World Cup in his hands, and Bobby Moore being carried aloft by his team mates, became a scene of national jubilation never repeated since. Alf was given the choice of kissing Nobby, or kissing the cup – he chose the cup!

The crowning glory for Suffolk football fans was to see their former manager display an unaccustomed show of emotion (though he would not take part in the lap of honour and even had to be persuaded to stay on the pitch after the final whistle). Old Stoneface, as a contemporary remarked, was lit up like the proverbial Christmas tree, all the more effective for the rarity factor.

When in 1974 the England team failed to live up to expectations Alf was sacked as manger. For a few short months he went to Birmingham City as caretaker manager but his heart had gone out of the game. In 1980 he became technical adviser to the Greek club Panathinaikos but was dismissed the following year. As England manager he lost only 17 of his 113 games yet was dismissed as yesterday's man and vilified by the merciless and punitive sports writers. He was the first England manager to have selection autonomy and, therefore, took the blame for any failure so was also the first to experience the biting venom of the tabloids. Ramsey had a cordial distrust of the press and, since people's reaction to him was often governed by his attitude towards them, the relationship was frequently strained. He did not suffer fools gladly and could be devastating in dealing with questions he felt foolish or impertinent.

Although knighted in 1967 the man who had changed the face of football and taken the national team to unprecedented world victory retired on a pension of £20 a week. Alf Ramsey had inspired his team to give England its greatest day in football history, yet praise stuck in the throats of the men in suits at the FA. Ramsey treated the FA members with tight-lipped courtesy but he had little patience with receptions or speeches and was very likely to skip a cocktail party if he could.

In 1991 Alf was reunited with his 1966 team before that year's

FA Cup final between his old team Spurs and Nottingham Forest. He conducted himself with the same degree of detached profess-ionalism that had marked his managerial career. No backslapping, chit-chat and definitely no champagne! Football had moved on from the heady days of the 1966 World Cup. Players were becoming stars on and off the pitch, earning salaries that the men of the post-war era never even dreamed about. It was a different game and a dif-ferent world.

Sir Alf Ramsey died in May 1999, aged seventy-nine. He had suffered from Alzheimer's and a stroke and died in a public hospital ward in Ipswich. The late Labour MP for Ipswich, Jamie Cann said: 'Sir Alf didn't come from Ipswich originally but he made it his home. He has lived here ever since, always just an ordinary, unas-suming man of the people, always helping charitable causes. He was well-loved and respected in the town and will be sadly missed.'

There had been no recognition in any form from the FA for his achievement or input into the game. It was as if Alf Ramsey's part in the 1966 World Cup phenomenon was forgotten. It was not until 1999 that Ipswich Town FC Supporters' Club rectified the situation and commissioned a statue of Sir Alf. In August 2000, former Town player Ray Crawford unveiled a life-size bronze statue of Sir Alf behind the north stand on the corner of Sir Alf Ramsey Way (previ-ously Portman Walk) and Portman Road. The ceremony was attended by his widow, Lady Ramsey, together with well-known football figures including players from the Ipswich Town of Sir Alf's days and representatives of the 1966 England team, including Sir Bobby Charlton.

Also present was the sculptor, Ipswich Town fan Sean Hedges-Quinn, who in 2002 was to sculpt another hero of Suffolk football, Sir Bobby Robson. Ipswich manager from 1969 to 1982, Bobby Robson was knighted in the 2002 Queen's Birthday Honours. He followed in Alf Ramsey's footsteps and took on the England man-ager's job in 1982, staying there for a gruelling eight years. Like Alf his relationship with the press was strained and he suffered from vicious tabloid onslaughts that, it would seem, go with the territory. Similarly, Sir Bobby was also not a native of Ipswich though he says they were both warmly welcomed into the Suffolk community, and writes:

> As well as being an exceptionally good studious player, Sir Alf was truly an outstanding manager. His success at Portman Road was absolutely phenomenal and of course, in achieving the ultimate triumph in 1966, winning the World Cup at Wembley, he wrote his name forever into English football history. Sir Alf was respected the world over. He was a football man at heart, innovative with a terrific work ethic possessing a great insight for the game. For me to follow in his footsteps, both at Club and International level, apart from being an almost impossible act to follow, filled me with immense pride. A unique football man with a deep love of the game, it will be difficult to see his like again.

Praise for Alf Ramsey comes from all quarters. Norman Burtenshaw, who spent eleven years as a league referee, taking in five appearances at Wembley (including the 1972 Cup Final), and a spell as an international referee, lives in Suffolk. For obvious reasons he rarely refereed at Ipswich, but knew Alf Ramsey by reputation. Talking to professional players and officials he heard, above all, of Alf's legendary discipline of the game and his players, both off and on the pitch:

> I think it was this discipline that made Alf confident enough to give that pronouncement about winning the World Cup in 1962. He'd seen other teams that were nowhere near as controlled as the England team. It was this, combined with a wide selection of top players, that won the Cup.

FIFTEEN

On the coast

IT WOULD BE surprising if many Suffolk stories did not derive from the fifty-odd miles of coastline, stretching from Lowestoft in the north to Felixstowe and the mouths of the rivers Orwell and Stour in the south. The very nature of the county is reliant on its historic coastal towns and villages and its proximity to mainland Europe. It has provided Suffolk with two of its major industries, fishing and the commercial ports of Ipswich and Felixstowe, plus tourism income in the small marinas and anchorages that cater for the sailing and boating fraternity. It has also been the cause of much despair and grief: many lives have been lost at sea, both of sailors and the men of the Suffolk Lifeboats. Such uncertainty instils a stoicism into the Suffolk character, which has its counterpart in the robust Martello towers, built in the early 1800s as a defence against the Napoleonic forces, which are dotted along its coast.

The Suffolk coast has borne the brunt of innumerable foreign invaders – from the earliest of times to the fierce naval battles against the Dutch in the seventeenth century. In the latter half of the century England and Holland came increasingly to blows over trade routes and fishing grounds and fought three separate wars between 1651 and 1674 off the coast of Suffolk. A fierce naval battle was fought off Lowestoft in 1665, when the English fleet sank or captured thirty-two Dutch ships, and two years later over a thousand Dutch soldiers and seaman landed on Suffolk's most conspicuous promontory, Landguard Fort at Felixstowe. This encounter was the last time a foreign force succeeded in landing on English soil.

Over the centuries those who live on this part of the coast have had a fluctuating relationship with Holland. In Southwold there are Dutch architectural styles which bear witness to its geographical proximity but there were many battles between the Dutch and the English, the home fleet at one time commanded by the Duke of York, later James II, who lived at Sutherland House. In 1672 the Battle of Sole Bay was fought off Southwold with the English and French (in one of the rare and brief periods when the two countries were allied) against the Dutch. The Dutch Admiral, De Ruyter, commanded ninety-one ships and surprised the English and French ships lying in Sole Bay on the morning of 28 May 1672. A fourteen-hour engagement commenced and the sound of gunfire was heard in London. Smoke engulfed the whole coast and even today an occasional cannon-ball from the battle is unearthed.

The squat, ovoid Martello towers that dot the Suffolk coastline were erected in the early nineteenth century when an invasion by Napoleon Bonaparte was considered likely. They stand thirty feet high with tapered walls, to deflect cannon fire, measuring up to thirteen feet thick on the seaward side and six feet facing inland. The bricks are bonded with hot lime mortar to give the walls a steel-like hardness. They were built on the most likely landing beaches and were named after a tower on Cape Mortella on the island of Corsica. Between 1805 and 1812, a string of 103 towers was built along the south and east coastline, eleven of them in Suffolk.

They were the idea of Captain William Ford who had seen the effectiveness of the fortified tower on the island of Corsica that had withstood heavy bombardment from the British in 1794. Ford made sketches of it and used them when planning fortifications against the feared French invasion. In the event, although England stood prepared, it never materialised.

Some bitterness was apparent in the county during those years, and allegations were even made that the local poet George Crabbe was a 'child and champion of Jacobinism'. His son refuted such charges:

> The truth is, that my father never was a politician . . . (but) nor did he ever conceal his opinion, that this war might have been avoided – and hence, in proportion to the weight of his local character, he gave offence to persons maintaining the diametrically opposite view of public matters at this peculiar crisis. As to the term 'Jacobin', I shall say only one word. None could have been less fitly applied to him at any period of his life. He was one of the innumerable good men who, indeed, hailed the beginning of the French Revolution, but who execrated its close.

After 1812 no more towers were built and, although Suffolk had stood ready to contain Bonaparte's invasion, not a shot was fired in anger. Some of the towers were dismantled, and the materials used elsewhere, but they still stand proud at Aldeburgh, Shingle Street, Alderton, Bawdsey, Felixstowe and Shotley Gate. At the height of the smuggling trade the towers were used by the Preventive Services, and when war with the French again seemed possible in the 1850s they were hastily prepared for use. In the First World War the Aldeburgh Martello tower was used to monitor the movements of German Zeppelins as they approached the East Anglian coast across the North Sea (then called the 'German Ocean'). Today several have been converted into elaborate – and highly unusual – homes.

War is not the only thing that shapes a county's coast, industry running a close second. Lowestoft owes its rich industrial past to one man, Samuel Morton Peto (1809–89), a Victorian entrepreneur, developer and railway contractor. In 1843 Lowestoft's future looked bleak. The company that owned the harbour, the Norwich and Lowestoft Navigation Company, had gone bankrupt and, because it had no rail link, the port was lagging behind. Peto promised the town a railway and was as good as his word: it became a reality in 1847 and almost immediately the Lowestoft fishing and shipping industries took off. Peto developed links with Denmark and steamships began bringing cattle, trade that is remembered today with Tonning Street, named after a Danish port, and Denmark Road. Hemp came from Russia, wool from Prussia, and oils, silks and wines from Italy, while suppliers closer to home were accessed: coal arrived from Tyneside and slate and stone from Wales.

Samuel Peto was a man of his age: a true entrepreneur who was not afraid to take risks, he had a vision of an industrial future that he was prepared to back with hard cash. In partnership with his cousin Thomas Grissel he built many major public buildings and monuments, including Nelson's column, three major London theatres, a prison, several hospitals and the London brick sewers which are still in use today. He purchased Somerleyton Hall in 1843 and masterminded its renaissance, although he was known for his eccentric tastes in architecture. He restored the Hall, rebuilt the local church and, during the 1840s and 1850s, built the estate village at Somerleyton.

Along Lowestoft's esplanade are two statues of Triton, who in Greek mythology was the son of Poseidon and Amphitrite and lived with them in a golden palace in the depths of the sea. He had the body of a man with the tail of a fish and rode the waves on horses and sea monsters. He carried a twisted conch shell into which he would blow either violently or gently to stir up or calm the waters. Peto had the statues sculpted as part of his plan for the enhancement of the promenade and sea front, designed to increase the tourist trade. The Lowestoft Tritons are shown holding the spiral shell that was used as Triton's trumpet and cornucopias disgorging sea urchins and other fruits of the sea.

The achievements of Peto's brilliant career, during which he built 750 miles of railway line in England and 2,300 miles abroad, included the Grand Trunk Railway of Canada. He became technically insolvent in 1866, being owed £1 million in unpaid debts. He had fourteen children, including Harold Peto, who inherited his father's love of building and became an architect, collector and connoisseur.

The two occupations of farming and fishing have sustained

Suffolk people for centuries, but for the towns and villages from Lowestoft down to Southwold the golden years of fishing climaxed in 1913, when 536,400 crans of herring (four baskets to a cran) were landed in Lowestoft harbour. There were some 1,500 drifters worked by 25,000 men and this was the largest catch of herring ever known and amounted to over half a million tons. Almost as much again of cod, plaice and other fish were brought in from the surrounding North Sea where the large number of boats meant that on most nights there would be mile upon mile of nets in close proximity. October 1913 was a memorable month for all, but that prodigious catch was never repeated.

Herring had been caught off the Suffolk coast since the tenth century, but in the 1870s hundreds of fishing boats from the Firth of Forth began leaving their Scottish harbour in pursuit of what Neil Gunn calls, in his novel about those days, 'the Silver Darlings'. They were following what they thought was the herring's migratory pattern down the Scottish coast to North Shields, Whitby and Scarborough, ending in East Anglia in October or November. It was assumed that the shoals moved gradually southwards, and hundred of boats and their crews 'followed the fishing' (although it has subsequently been established that each area yields its own characteristic variety of herring).

The fleet's arrival was immediately followed by an 'invasion' of Scottish fishergirls who shadowed the boats south each year. Special trains would bring a virtual army of women from Scotland to gut and pack the fish caught by the fleet. By the early 1900s, when the power and scope of the sailing vessels had been boosted by growing numbers of steam drifters, the Suffolk harbours would be home to around five thousand Scottish fishergirls for several weeks. Some of them came back year after year, eventually marrying and settling in Suffolk. They came accompanied by wooden boxes or trunks containing each woman's personal belongings. There was no mistaking them in the streets as they went around in groups, wearing brightly coloured woollen jumpers, thick skirts and heavy leathers to protect them in their exposed working conditions. At work they wore oily aprons and coloured shawls.

When they were not at work they were usually knitting. They went for walks on their days off and on Sundays, knitting as they went. In 1903 the *Gorleston Times* reported:

> It is interesting to see the newly arrived Scotch specials disgorging their squadrons of red-haired, ruddy-cheeked passengers . . . Their faces are aglow with health, their hair, innocent of covering, neatly and fashionably done, and with good warm clothing in strong contrast to the shoddy dress of their southern sisters, they present the very embodiment of strength and comeliness. They are happy, too, despite their arduous, unpleasant work – ever singing and busily knitting as they take their walks.

In David Butcher's *Following the Fleet*, Annie Watt (1892–1978) tells how she left her Peterhead home each year to go south:

> We used tae come down by train. In the old days it only cost 30 shillings return. Ye never went to sleep. All the guttin' crews would be singing and dancing. We used tae have small spirit lamps and make tea in the train. Oh, it was fun. Ye never felt the time.

Annie eventually married a Lowestoft man and worked for many seasons in the gutting crews.

To avoid cutting themselves the girls would wrap their fingers with bits of rag: it was no joke for salt to be continuously worked into open wounds and gloves were still a thing of the future. The coopers salted the fish to make them less slippery. Annie and her gang would each gut fifty to sixty herrings a minute. Working on piece rates in teams of three (two girls gutting and one packing) they could handle around 3,000 fish in an hour – nearly one fish per second.

The women lived in guesthouses and 'digs' up and down the coast. Some of the landladies were better than others and some of their lodgers cleaner than others. At the start of the season the landladies cleared the rooms of furniture and carpets and lined the walls with brown paper in case the girls were careless about taking off their dirty clothes. After long stretches of up to nine or ten hours gutting and packing herrings in cold weather, their hands red and stinging from the brine and cracked by the salt, they were often too tired even to take their coats off. They used their boxes as chairs and brought with them only what they could carry.

In the late 1940s and early 1950s it was a great attraction to go to the harbours where the Scottish 'lassies' worked. School parties and family outings were taken to watch them wield the short gutting knife, making an incision in the throat of the fish, withdrawing the gill and long gut with a single stroke. They sang as they worked, the Scottish accents often incomprehensible to the Suffolk ear but all part of the atmosphere.

On Sundays the sheds were eerily quiet. Due to strong religious convictions, the fishergirls never worked on Sundays and few Scottish skippers would work or put to sea on the Sabbath, often to their detriment if Sunday was a good fishing day. Religion, though, was a bond between many of the Scots and the Lowestoft Nonconformists, notably the influential Mobbs family. One of these, William Mobbs, has gone down in folklore.

William Mobbs was a butcher by trade and in the late nine-teenth century was one of those whose business was boosted by the influx of the Scottish fleet. One day a group of Scottish skippers made their way to the butcher's shop. With set and sombre faces they told him that they were unable to pay his bill. Their spokesman said:

> You know what has happened, Mr Mobbs. All us Scottish fishermen sold our fish through one seller. Now he's gone off with our money. Our vessels are up-river, the other side of the bridge, and the bridgemen have orders not to open to let us through because we cannot pay our harbour dues. Tradesmen in the town have come to us for settlement, and we cannot pay. We are all your customers for meat, and we thought it only right to call and tell you so that you can take what action you think fit.

William Mobbs eyed them shrewdly, then said, 'Yes, I will take proper action. Haven't I seen some you worshipping beside me in the Bethel?'

Many had indeed attended the Sailor's and Fishermen's Bethel, a Free Evangelical church not bound by formality, where the Nonconformists among them were guaranteed a welcome. Many Scottish skippers flew special 'Bethel' pennants at the masthead to show they had taken a pledge not to break the Sabbath. William told the men to produce the bills they owed him and, to their astonishment, tore them up. 'Now I have no legal hold over you', he said, 'but if, at any time, any of you can afford to repay me, I rely on your honour to do so. If you don't, it will never prosper you.'

The men were grateful and asked if there was anything they could do in return to show their appreciation. In reply William gave them a note for the Harbourmaster's Office and asked them to deliver it forthwith. The Harbour Clerk saw the men approach and feared trouble. He could not let their boats out of the harbour until they paid the dues. The spokesmen handed him William's note, which he read aloud: 'Please release the boats of these men and I will be personally responsible for their harbour dues.'

William Mobbs's word was good enough for him and without delay the boats were released. As they passed through the Lynn-Wells Deeps the boats were close enough for their crew to speak to one another, and they remembered that a shoal of herrings was caught around that point of the coast some years ago, long after the regular shoals had gone. 'We're going home penniless and in debt, with nothing to give our families when we get home,' said the spokesmen. 'Shall we shoot our nets? We may get a few herrings to eat, anyway.' The nets were shot and when they were hauled they brought with them a heavy catch of fish. They hauled again, and caught more fish which they sold ashore. Some of the boats made as much as £100 at a time when herrings were rarely seen off that part of the coast.

A few weeks later William Mobbs was astounded to arrive at his office one morning to find a pile of letters, each bearing a Scottish postmark. Letter after letter contained a cheque from each of the skippers, for slightly more than was due. Each man had worked out the interest and added it to the amount. Each year thereafter, the skippers who returned to Suffolk visited William Mobbs, who went down in history as 'the butcher with the heart of gold'.

By the 1930s the numbers of fish were in serious decline and the bigger boats with bigger nets devastated what remained of the natural herring stocks. In the 1880s the fishing industry had worked on a limited scale with boats powered by sail, which needed 50,000 men to make modest but profitable catches. Then came the steam boats, and the heady days of 1913, when the record catch was made by just half the number of men needed in the days of sail. This was followed by diesel power, reducing further the number of jobs but having the capacity to trawl vast areas of the seas. Hundreds of steam drifters were broken up, or abandoned. The plentiful stocks were eventually wiped out and the fishing grounds irreversibly depleted.

By the end of the 1950s fishing off the Suffolk coast was hardly an industry at all, and such trawlers as there were concentrated their efforts on cod, haddock and plaice, until Britain entered the European Economic Community and gave away the last of the valuable fishing grounds.

SIXTEEN

For the love of Will

THE SAGA OF Margaret Catchpole has been told and retold to generations of Suffolk people and is one of the county's best-known stories, all the more poignant because it is true. It is a tale of love, betrayal, misfortune and dogged courage, which took place in the late eighteenth century at a time when smugglers ruled the local economies and thus touched the lives of everyone. Margaret was an extraordinary young woman from a humble background who fell in love with a smuggler, became a criminal by default and ended up a prisoner on a transportation ship bound for Australia.

Margaret was born in 1773 into a typical working-class Suffolk family in Nacton, on the outskirts of Ipswich, where her father Jonathan was a farm labourer. She was one of six children and shared with her father his love of the huge Suffolk cart-horses used on farms in those days. When she was barely five years old, her mother would send her out to the fields with her father's lunch. Jonathan would throw her up onto the neck of one of the horses where she would sit happily while he rested and the horses snuffled in their nosebags and shook their manes against the rich chesnut colouring (see page 69 for an explanation of the spelling of the Suffolk Punch's colour) of their shiny, sleek coats. She clung on tight as he set them to work and the sight of the small, fearless child, her hands twisted in the heavy mane, riding bareback became a familiar one.

She learned to call 'Whoah!' and 'Gee-up!' and rode with a confidence and enthusiasm that belied her years and sex. When evening came she would ride the leading horse home and take the team down to the pond edge where they would throw off the dust and fatigue of the day in the cool water.

The child grew into a handsome young woman, bright and quick-witted, who looked after her ailing elder sister and younger brother. Margaret had little or no education, as none in the Catchpole household could read or write. At fourteen she went into service as a dairymaid, where her capable manner and capacity for hard work endeared her, not unnaturally, to her employer, Mr Nathaniel Southgate of Great Bealings. But her mother soon needed her back at Nacton: her sister was dying.

Aged sixteen, Margaret was strong but also slim, with a pleasant, honest face, and was beginning to turn heads. The Catchpoles were neighbours to the Cracknell family and were as close as they could be, the men working on the same farm and the women reliant on one another in a remote, rural backwater. Shortly after Margaret's return home from service, Susan Cracknell asked her to be godmother to her daughter. One Stephen Laud, a relative of Mrs Cracknell, was to be the other sponsor. Stephen was a famous boatman who piloted the ferry with great skill between Langer Fort, now called Landguard Fort, and Harwich. A widower, Stephen had only one son – William, called Will – who was apprenticed as a boat-builder.

Young Will Laud was particularly bright and had an abiding love of the sea. He studied navigation with Mr Crabbe, a brother of the celebrated poet, who said he was the quickest lad as a mathematician he ever knew. But it was obvious to everyone that Will would never build boats, he would only sail them. He struck up a friendship with a Captain Bargood, master and owner of several ships then trading along the coast and across to Holland.

By the day of the christening, Stephen and Will Laud had had several days of deep and animated conversation. Twenty-year-old Will was trying to persuade his father to let him leave the boat-yard and go to sea. Captain Bargood had offered him a job and though in his heart knew he would take it, he nevertheless wanted his father's blessing.

Stephen gave in and they travelled to Nacton in harmony, though Will had other things on his mind. He had Margaret Catchpole on his mind, though they had not met. He remembered hearing of an incident, when Margaret was fourteen, when she had ridden a pony full speed from Nacton to Ipswich to summon a doctor to attend a friend's mistress. It had been the talk of the neighbourhood and had caused much embarrassment to Margaret. Riding a horse bareback for miles and through the crowded streets of Ipswich was not seemly, even for a farm worker's daughter. Soon afterwards she had gone into service with Mr Southgate and had vowed never to ride again, praying that the incident might be forgotten.

The spark of love that flew between Margaret Catchpole and Will Laud was ignited the day they first laid eyes on each other and was never extinguished. It was fanned into a true and enduring bond between them, though destiny decreed that it should not be long-lived or happy. Their time together was destined to be brief, fraught with danger, and subject to the whim of fate.

Will was hard to resist. He was intelligent and handsome, with a quick and ready smile. He could tell a story or sing a song with animation and charm. Romantic tales of the high seas and a sparkling, unknown world beyond the drudgery of farm work won him instant friends among the men at the gathering. The women watched knowingly as Will stole Margaret's heart and, aware of his roving spirit, feared for her future.

Will became a regular visitor to the Catchpole home until Captain Bargood summoned him to Felixstowe to take up his employment. Although loath to leave Margaret he was eager to begin his new life at sea. An 'arrangement' existed between them, to the delight of both families. Everyone except Margaret's older sister approved of Will. She had a foreboding that he would not bring

Margaret happiness. With her dying breath she told Margaret that Will would never marry her and made her promise that she would never be his, except that they were married.

In those days the Suffolk coast was a haven of opportunity for smugglers who landed their goods at points along the beaches and river inlets which were just across the water from Holland and the Low Countries. Tax was heavy on luxury goods and the saving well worth the risk of being caught by the English Preventive Service or the Dragoons. A pound of tea could be bought in Holland for ten pence, but the duty in England was more than twice that sum. Brandy was forty-five pence a gallon and smugglers could sell it for fifteen pence and make a profit.

Smugglers were considered folk heroes who pitted their wits against the Revenue officers whose job it was to track them down and find their hiding places, a job made all the more difficult by the connivance of locals eager to buy cut-price tea, tobacco and brandy. Students of Rudyard Kipling's *A Smuggler's Son* will recall the lines:

If you wake at midnight, and hear a horse's feet,
Don't go drawing back the blind, or looking in the street,
Them that asks no questions isn't told a lie.
Watch the wall, my darling, while the Gentlemen go by!
   Five-and twenty ponies,
   Trotting through the dark –
   Brandy for the Parson,
   'Baccy for the Clerk;
   Laces for a lady; letters for a spy,
   And watch the wall, my darling, while the Gentlemen go by!

More than one Suffolk ghost story is the result of creative invention designed to keep the curious at home. Certain roads and lanes were said to be the haunt of ferocious black hounds which terrorised the imaginations of those who felt safer behind locked front doors while the 'gentlemen' went by.

In almost every village and hamlet along the coast can still be found a cottage named 'Smugglers'. There are other places famous for being the haunt of smugglers, like the Cat House, at Woolverstone, on the south bank of the river Orwell. Its end walls were painted to look like church windows and a white cat was placed on a windowsill as a signal to the smugglers bringing contraband to a safe house.

Pubs, like the White Hart at Blythburgh and the Queen's Head at Blyford, that were conveniently placed between the shore and the routes to inland 'markets', were frequented, while others like the Crown at Snape had a secret room accessible only by a trapdoor. Churches were favourite hideouts: at Rishangles a deep hole was found under the pulpit and discovered to be the entrance to a tunnel and a well-used storage site for Dutch kegs and bottles of spirits. Booty was hidden under more than one altar cloth, provided the parson got his brandy. The Catchpole and Cracknell families were aware of battles fought nightly between the Revenue men and the smugglers in the lanes and byways leading inland from Felixstowe to Ipswich. But it was the smugglers of Sizewell Gap who were feared more than most, together with the notorious Hadleigh gang that ran booty from the Gap, via Semer, inland to Hadleigh. They were not above murder and violence to protect their merchandise.

Sizewell was a forsaken hamlet, with only one farmstead, and because of that beloved of the smugglers. 'Interlopers', anyone outside the gang, could be buried up to their necks in shingle and left in the isolated hamlet where few ventured. Many a Revenue man was found thrust headfirst into a rabbit warren, his wrists and ankles fastened so that he could not wriggle free. The Revenue men were backed by Dragoons many of whom were killed or injured in the course of their duties.

Will Laud knew about the smugglers – how could he not? – but as he left Nacton for Felixstowe he travelled with a heavy heart. Captain Bargood had offered him command of a brig, and he knew why. His father knew, too, and had warned Will about the kind of life he would lead if he gave up an honest job in the boatyard to take to the high seas as captain of a smuggler vessel. But Will told himself it was only temporary, until he could afford to marry Margaret and settle down in an honest job.

His first trip was to Holland, the return cargo gin. Captain Bargood let his men bargain on their own account for snuff, tobacco, linen and anything else they could procure. Will got one-sixth of the profit for his first year which, by his reckoning, meant that if he could make something on the side he and Margaret could be married in a year. The risk he weighed to be small. Captain Bargood's legitimate business perfectly masked his illicit smuggling operations, and cheap brandy soon made friends in the county. The black economy was empowered by the resentment many felt against the high taxes. The smugglers enjoyed local support – shepherds would drive their flocks over the smugglers' tracks, and farriers could be persuaded to reverse a horse's shoes to confuse the Dragoons. Besides, he reasoned, he could win Margaret over by sending her fine linen and furs. If she took them she could say nothing.

His first parcel was delivered to the Catchpoles' cottage on a solemn day. They had just returned from the funeral of Margaret's elder sister when a roughly spoken man with a weather-beaten face handed her a package. Inside were silks and shawls, caps and lace, ribbons and gloves, together with packets of tea, coffee, tobacco and snuff. Margaret knew who had sent them and what it meant. Will had joined the smugglers.

The man left empty-handed, in spite of Margaret's insistence that he must return the parcel. She felt compromised and hurt: if she handed the goods to the Revenue she would implicate Will, but if she kept them she and her family could be in serious trouble. But Mrs Cracknell had fewer scruples and successfully disposed of the goods for a tidy and welcome profit, split between the two families.

As Captain Bargood had foreseen, Will made a daring captain. He sailed close to the wind in more ways than one as gradually his exploits became legendary and his notoriety grew. Cargo and after cargo was landed on Bawdsey beach and stored in a cave below the cliffs before being run inland and on to contacts throughout the county. Sometimes a farmer would discover a horse to be missing from its stable or field, needed urgently by the smugglers for a night-time run, and casks of gin or packets of linen left in its stead.

Will was now known as Captain Laud and although he had

not been to see Margaret for some time their names were linked and her family began to stand in the shadow of danger. More and more goods found their way to Margaret's door and time after time she rejected them, though Mrs Cracknell's business grew prosperous. Stephen Laud lost his job as ferryman at Landguard Fort and was accused of complicity in his son's illegal activities. Jonathan Catchpole, too, left his job and the family moved to another cottage on Nacton Heath.

It was only a matter of time before Will had his first serious encounter with the Revenue men. A rumour was put about that the Sizewell gang was planning a night run from Walton Marshes to Woodbridge, so that the Revenue men and their attendant Dragoons would be diverted. Laud and his men would be at Bawdsey cliffs, running stored booty inland. They thought it had worked, but the ruse was discovered. Led by Lieutenant Edward Barry, the coastguard sprang out as Laud and his men began to load the contraband and a fierce fight ensued. Three of the crew were killed and others badly wounded. Soon only Lieutenant Barry and Will were left to fight it out, man to man, with swords. Laud wounded Edward Barry and would have finished him off, but the Lieutenant rallied and caught Will across his head, cutting through his hat and across his forehead. Will fell to the ground and Barry thought he had killed him, as he would have done if his life not been saved by John Luff, the captain's mate. Badly wounded, Barry staggered forward only to be attacked again by John Luff who then threw Will over his shoulder and made off into the night.

Will was taken to his father's cottage near the ruins of Walton Castle and, thinking he was dying, Stephen Laud sent for Margaret.

Captain Laud did not die. Margaret nursed him back to health, ever hopeful that she could persuade him to give up his life of crime. But as much as he loved her, he was too deeply involved with Bargood. Though he promised her that he would seek employment as an honest trader on a Dutch vessel he had no such intention. Within hours of leaving his father's cottage, fully recovered, he was back with John Luff and the crew at Bawdsey cliffs. He no longer called himself Laud, but became Captain Hudson.

Thinking that Will was in safe and legal employment, Margaret took a new job at Priory Farm, Downham Reach, where she met John Barry whose brother Edward had almost killed Will. John was both industrious and enterprising and had good prospects at Priory Farm. He knew about Margaret and Will Laud, but from what his brother had said he supposed Laud dead and had no reason to connect him with the exploits of Captain Hudson. He fell hopelessly in love with Margaret Catchpole and asked her to marry him.

Margaret did not mean to tell John that Will was not dead, but she had no other way of refusing his persistent offers of marriage. But when he heard, Will accused her of betrayal and began to lead her a merry dance, calling to see her in the various houses where she was in service, and even trying to kidnap her and take her with him to Holland. She moved from one job to another as gradually her spirit was sapped and she despaired of ever being married. Then she entered the service of John Cobbold, an Ipswich brewer, where she struck up an enduring friendship with his young, and second, wife Elizabeth. There was plenty to do, as the brewer already had fourteen children and looked forward to more. Soon after entering their service she had saved one of the children – Henry Gallant Cobbold, the fourteenth child of John's first marriage – from drowning, which gave her a special place in the house. Margaret worked hard and in her few spare hours Elizabeth Cobbold taught her the rudiments of reading and writing and she settled into the comfortable routine of the Cobbold household at Cliff Brewery.

Then a letter arrived. Will was in London and – at last – waiting to make her his wife.

All reason left Margaret as she planned how to reach London. In a moment of madness, and longing to see Will and be married at last, she resolved to take one of John Cobbold's carriage horses. Disguised as a man she would ride to London where, not wishing to steal from her employer, she would sell the horse and send the money back to Ipswich. She rode like the wind, the years falling away as she became the young and capricious Margaret

Catchpole on her way to meet Will Laud, seaman, adventurer and the love of her life. It was seventy miles to London and she made it in less than nine hours.

Alas for Margaret, the horse was recognised as stolen. She was arrested at Aldgate in May 1797 and committed to Newgate Prison. Two months later she was removed to Ipswich Gaol. Horse stealing was punishable by death in those days and at the Bury Assizes she was condemned to death by hanging. Elizabeth Cobbold visited her in gaol, and messages came from many old friends, but from Will she heard nothing. Margaret knew she was compromised beyond hope and would, in due course, forfeit her life in the final proof of her love for Will, whom she would never see again.

But she was wrong. Arrested for debt, Will had ended up in the same Ipswich prison as Margaret, though no one knew that the sailor in the debtors' prison was the notorious Captain Laud. By chance she was sent to take some washing to that part of the gaol reserved for the debtors and there caught a glimpse of a sailor. She instantly recognised him and over the next few months they were able to see each other briefly and exchange a few words. Finally the day came when Will told her of his impending release. His debts had been paid and it was their last chance to be together. She must escape and they would travel to Holland where they would be married.

In March 1800 Margaret Catchpole began to plan her escape from Ipswich gaol. She had very little to lose. 'I shall be waiting for you outside the wall, never fear,' said Will, 'and will have a sailor's jacket and hat for your disguise.' They would go to Sudbourne. From there it would be easy to make their way through the inlets and marsh tracks that the smugglers had made their own, to a boat waiting on the Orford shore.

As a trusted prisoner it was easy for Margaret to get the clotheshorse and linen line needed for her escape from the prison laundry. She must choose a day when the governor took prisoners from Ipswich to the Bury Assizes, taking most of the prison staff with him. On 25 March 1800 Margaret hid in an empty cell and at midnight made good her escape. Climbing up the wooden clotheshorse she threw the line over a small break in the wall's defences and landed outside the prison. As she fell onto the earth the chimes of St Clement's church struck midnight and in the lane beside St Helen's stood Will. There was no time for a reunion; Margaret changed quickly into the sailor's uniform and they set out for Sudbourne travelling quickly under the cover of darkness. Speed was of the essence and they kept to the lanes they knew were free of prying eyes.

As the fugitives hurried towards Orford, all hell was let loose in Ipswich. On discovering Margaret gone the prison governor's wife sent a message to her husband at Bury St Edmunds. People from the town began to arrive to see the break in the wall and crowds gathered as the authorities began hammering wanted notices across the town. A reward of £20 was offered:

> Escaped from the County Goal, at Ipswich, last night, or early this Morning – Margaret Catchpole, a convict . . . She is about 28 years of age, swarthy complexion – very dark eyes and hair – hard favoured – about 5 feet 2 inches high, and escaped in a convict's dress, which she has, probably, changed, and may be disguised in men's apparel. Whoever shall apprehend the said Margaret Catchpole, so she may be brought to justice, will be entitled to a reward of twenty pounds, granted by Act of Parliament.

Elizabeth Cobbold was summoned and was distressed to hear that Margaret had known the prisoner to be Captain Laud but had not told her. Back in Ipswich the governor sent word to the Preventive Men: once apprised of the true identity of his sailor debtor he knew where to look for his escaped prisoner. A certain Captain Edward Barry had lately been successful in securing the arrest of several smuggling gangs and by chance Barry had command of a Revenue cutter on patrol in the river Alde. Edward Barry and Will Laud were about to meet for the second time.

Will and Margaret made good time to Sudbourne and their confidence grew with every mile. There had been no time for Margaret to press Will on his promise that they would be married before leaving England, but she trusted that they would begin a new life together in Holland as man and wife. Marriage on board ship was by no means unusual and he had, she decided, arranged everything. It was still dark when they left Sudbourne and they hurried across the marshes towards Orford.

Captain Edward Barry was a man possessed of a strong sense of duty. He knew right from wrong and was one of the most feared of the Preventive Men. His duel with Will Laud had passed into folklore but the fact that Will had survived, and in doing so thwarted his brother's chances of marrying Margaret, still rankled with him. When he heard that the runaways were headed towards Orford he smiled with wry satisfaction. There were debts to settle and this time he was determined that he, and the law, would prevail. What might happen to Margaret he pushed to the back of his mind, as he knew that his brother was still in love with her and would find it hard to forgive him if anything happened to her.

Hand in hand Will and Margaret stood on the Orford shore and watched as their boat rode the waves towards them in the faint early-morning light. It was a blustery day but the storm clouds had lifted and there was promise of a good crossing. Margaret was so happy she could not speak. Will had promised to marry her and take an honest job, the two things she had longed for since the day they had first met. But as the boat drew nearer a second vessel hove into sight. It approached from the river side of the Orford spit and Captain Barry saw his prey long before Will realised he was there.

Margaret, however, saw the second vessel and with a cry she ran towards the sea, pulling Will along, determined to swim to their waiting boat. But the waves were too strong and Will pulled her back onto the sand, both of them soaked to the skin with cold sea water. They clung to each other, knowing it was all over, though Will held her with one hand and with the other felt in his coat for his gun.

Captain Barry approached, his gun pointing at Will: 'Give her up, Will! She's a felon under sentence of death and shall be returned to gaol.' Will raised his gun – in surrender or in anger will never be known – and Captain Barry took aim and fired. William Laud, sailor, smuggler, adventurer and lover fell back and died, his body slumped against that of the loyal, faithful and badly used Margaret Catchpole, who had risked all for his love. As Captain Barry advanced toward her she screamed and fainted, all hope gone. More dead than alive, Margaret Catchpole was taken back to Ipswich gaol and put in solitary confinement.

It was a very different Margaret who next greeted Elizabeth Cobbold. She had lost her former spirit and grieved miserably for Will. She confessed everything and repented at having caused the Cobbolds so much trouble. But Elizabeth came to her rescue again. Margaret was to go before the Assizes once more but this time the Cobbolds would intervene on her behalf. They would plead that she was influenced unduly by Laud and ask that the sentence of death be commuted to deportation.

And so it was that in 1801 Margaret became one of the 24,960 women convicts transported to Australia throughout the transportation period 1787–1868. Desolate at leaving her native Suffolk, and her family, she wrote to Elizabeth from her cell in Ipswich gaol on 25 May 1801:

> I am sorry I have to inform you this Bad newes that I am going away on wedensday next or Thursday at the longest so I hav taken the Liberty my good Ladey of trobling you with a few Lines as it will Be the Larst time I ever shall trobell you in this sorrofoll Confinement my sorrows are very grat to think I must Be Banished out of my owen Countreay and from all my Dearest friendes for ever it is very hard inded for anyone to think on it and much moor for me to enduer the hardship of it honred madam.

Margaret and two other women prisoners were taken to Portsmouth and seen safely onto the convict ship bound for Botany Bay. Conditions on board were atrocious but on arrival in Sydney she was assigned as a servant to a government official and two years later had proved so hardworking and resourceful that she was sent to Richmond Hill to act as midwife to a Mrs Rouse, a farmer's wife. There she put into practice her childhood knowledge of farming and was soon running the farm.

She was pardoned in 1814 but remained in Australia where she opened a general store and acted as the local midwife and nurse. She died in 1819, probably from pneumonia after making a midwifery call in bad weather, and was buried in St Peter's Church, Richmond, New South Wales.

Margaret's legacy is not just her story of love and betrayal, but also the many letters that she wrote to Elizabeth Cobbold and to her surviving relatives in Suffolk, giving graphic accounts of daily life in the colony. She wrote about the aborigines, and about such disasters as the Hawkesbury River floods and thousands of other daily occurrences that showed her to have a keen mind and an ability to observe her surroundings and the people she met.

She wrote in her phonetic hand, perfectly illustrating the beautiful rhythm of her speech, which in itself is an invaluable written witness of the Suffolk dialect as she spoke it. She wrote about the local wildlife, especially the snakes which she said were '12 feet Long and as big as your thy and maney very Daingress things'. She sent souvenirs back to Ipswich, including the stuffed lyre bird that is still in Ipswich Museum.

The letters that Margaret wrote to Elizabeth Cobbold passed, in due course, to her son, the Revd Richard Cobbold. Richard, the second youngest of John Cobbold's twenty children, was born at Ipswich in 1797 and educated at Bury St Edmunds, before becoming a curate in Ipswich. He became rector at the north Suffolk village of Wortham in 1824 and stayed for fifty years. He was an artist, poet, novelist, essayist and diarist and many of his original paintings and essays formed the basis of a book entitled *The Biography of a Victorian Village* by the Suffolk writer Ronald Fletcher. In 1845 he wrote *The History of Margaret Catchpole, A Suffolk Girl*, a novel based on the letters and his mother's memoirs. Since then it has been reprinted in numerous volumes and is to Suffolk what *Lorna Doone* is to the West Country. The 'Margaret' of Richard Cobbold's novel married, and had children, but the real Margaret did not, in spite of several offers.

Only a few years after Richard Cobbold and his wife celebrated their golden wedding he and his wife died within two days of each other and were buried at the same time.

Elizabeth Cobbold was also a poet and at one time an actress. She is immortalised as Charles Dickens's 'Mrs Leo Hunter' and no doubt met the writer during one of his visits to Suffolk. She dedicated a volume of verse entitled *Six Narrative Poems* to the artist Sir Joshua Reynolds, evidently by permission. Elizabeth gave her husband six children, and it is hardly surprising that the name Cobbold was, and still is, much in evidence in Ipswich and the county of Suffolk. She died in 1824 and her husband John outlived her by eleven years.

SEVENTEEN

Churchyard tales

THERE ARE AROUND 600 churches, or ruins of churches, in Suffolk and almost 300 are mentioned in the Suffolk Little Domesday survey gathered by the commissioners of William the Conqueror in 1086. Many replaced older wooden Saxon edifices and since each church has been added to or altered over anything up to a thousand years, each one is unique. Every church has a story to tell of adventurers and landed and royal families. As often as not, a famous man or woman is buried in its precinct.

Among the poets and men of letters buried in Suffolk is Edward FitzGerald, born in 1809 at Bredfield, near Woodbridge. FitzGerald is famous for his letters to his friends and for his translation of the *Rubaiyat of Omar Khayyam*. He was also something of a boating enthusiast and consorted with the fishing folk, one Joseph 'Posh' Fletcher in particular, a Lowestoft fisherman some thirty years his junior. 'Posh' skippered FitzGerald's boat *Scandal* named, said the poet, after 'the staple commodity of Woodbridge'. FitzGerald died in 1883 and is buried in the family mausoleum at St Michael and All Angels Church at Boulge. Though currently in a dire state of repair, it is visited by people from all over the world. Roses planted on his grave were brought from Sheik Omar Khayyam's home at Nishapur in Persia.

Modern additions to Suffolk's churches are memorials to those who served in the military forces of two world wars. No church is without its list of parish sons, whether three or thirty-three, and almost all churchyards have a war memorial. In East Anglia, and Suffolk in particular, the American servicemen of the Second World War are also remembered in the communities in which they served and lived. Near Horham church is a memorial to the 95th Bomb Group and at Great Ashfield there is a memorial nave and book of remembrance in the church and a plaque in the churchyard. There are memorials, too, in Elveden, Lavenham and Stradishall churches. A flag and plaque in Clopton Church commemorates the 493rd Bomb Group that operated out of Debach, and at Stradbroke there is a flag in memory of the three Bomb Groups at Horham. At Sudbury, in addition to a plaque on the town hall, there is a memorial stone at both the church and airfield.

Those who endowed the churches, or served as rector or vicar, are remembered in memorial brasses, engravings and tombs both inside the buildings and in the churchyards, and their stories live on in books and church guides. Such a story concerns the Cantrell family of St Gregory's, Hemingstone.

Soon after Henry VIII's Reformation, when the national church became Protestant instead of Roman Catholic, the Catholic families of sixteenth-century England were persecuted and forced to conform to the new forms of religious service. The old-established Cantrell family of Hemingstone was one that retained its loyalty to the old religion. One of their number, William Cantrell, was a trustee of the Catholic Thomas, Duke of Norfolk, who was executed in 1572 for attempting to marry Mary, Queen of Scots. (William Cantrell has an imposing tomb inside the church, decorated with painted shields.) In post-Reformation Suffolk their home and farmland was liable to confiscation if the family did not attend Protestant services in St Gregory's Church.

The law did not, however, state that worshippers had to be in the body of the church, only that they must attend and have sight of the altar. Ralph's idea was simple: he would construct a porch on the south wall of the church and have a hole knocked through so that he could see into the nave without actually being in it. Every Sunday the Cantrell family would trudge up the hill from Stonewall Farm (then known as Wealden Farm) to St Gregory's to observe the service through a tiny, oblong peephole (or 'squint') that can be seen in the church, and the south porch is now used as a vestry.

The Cantrell family left Suffolk for the Americas in the eighteenth century and many of its descendants come to visit Hemingstone, the one-time family seat.

A Suffolk man with more flexible principles was the colourful Bishop John Bale (1495–1563) who was born in the area of Cove (now Covehithe), just north of Southwold, and whose name is forever associated with the ruin of St Andrew's. There is some dispute as to which of the Cove villages was his precise birthplace, but popular opinion has it as Covehithe where, as a young man, John Bale would have worshipped at the imposing church when it was less than a hundred years old and at that time one of the largest in Suffolk.

Bale was a pupil at a Carmelite convent in Norwich, where he learned to be a zealous Roman Catholic, but he went to Cambridge in 1529 where he came under the influence of a group of ardent reformers, among them Thomas Cranmer. He converted to Protestantism.

John Bale rejected the idea of a celibate clergy and laid aside his monastic habit to marry a woman known only as Dorothy. The couple moved to Thorndon, near Eye, where he immediately began preaching controversial and anti-Catholic sermons, at a time when Catholicism was still the English religion. In 1534 he was summoned before the Archbishop of York where he stood accused of inflammatory preaching of an anti-Catholic nature against the invocation of saints. One saint in particular was singled out for his bile, and earned him the nickname 'Bilious Bale'. He ridiculed the curative claims made on behalf of the eleventh-century patron saint of farm workers, St Walstan, and indulged his tendency to the erotic by comparing him to Priapus (a Greek god represented as a carica-ture of the human form, grotesquely misshapen, with an enormous phallus). The legend of St Walstan attributes restorative powers to the water of St Walstan's Well but Bale misrepresented claims of miracu-lous healing by suggesting that pilgrims believed the water would 'restore men's prevy parts'. In his *English Votaries* he wrote: '. . . that both Men and Beastes which had lost their Prevy Parts, had newe Members again restored to them, by this Walstane. Marke thys kyne of Myracles, for your Learnynge, I thynke Ye have seldome readde the lyke.'

By 1540 John Bale had made so many enemies by his outspoken sermons and unorthodox behaviour that, together with Dorothy and their several children, he was forced to leave Suffolk for Germany. One contemporary description speaks of his 'rude vigour of expres-sion', and 'want of good taste and moderation'.

Thereafter the Bale family led an adventurous life, moving eventually to Ireland, an uninspired choice since most of the clergy there remained faithful to Catholicism and, therefore, to the practice of clerical celibacy and the invocation of saints, concepts that Bale regularly rejected from the pulpit. When Henry VIII's new Protestant religion was fully established Bale returned to England, only to have to flee again when the Catholic Queen Mary was crowned.

During one of his sojourns in England he was created bishop and began writing plays, among them *Kynge Johan*, written about 1548. *Kynge Johan* marks a literary transition between the old morality plays and the new historical drama of the Reformation in which Bale portrayed King John as a champion of English rites against the Church of Rome. The original manuscript was lost for many years, but was discovered in the 1830s among the corporation papers at Ipswich, where it had almost certainly been performed.

At the end of a controversial and eventful life Bishop Bale finally settled at Canterbury under the Protestant Queen Elizabeth and died there in 1563. If any memorial existed to Bishop John Bale at Covehithe it has long since disappeared. In the seventeenth century the enormous church became too much for the tiny community of Covehithe and they dismantled it leaving only the tower. A smaller church was built within the shell of the old one but the spectacular 100-foot-high tower and the walls of the ruined church still stand, though for how long is uncertain. That part of the coast is vulnerable to erosion and inch by inch the sandy cliffs are crumbling down onto the shore. Soon it will follow the lost city of Dunwich into the sea.

Once the ancient town of Dunwich was an important centre with a busy harbour, hospitals, a king's palace, a mint and as many as ten churches, several chapels, convents and monasteries. By 1350 parts of the town had been washed away and piece by piece the rest crumbled until the great storms which raged along the coast between 1680 and 1740 gradually ate into the cliffs and took what was left. In 1919 the last part of the Church of Dunwich All Saints tumbled into the sea.

Fishermen talk of the sound of church bells that can be heard on a still night, and the lowing of cattle from the lost pastures that once surrounded Dunwich. Bishop Bale would have known Dunwich, which in its day had seen countless numbers of pilgrims arriving from Europe to seek out the saints and shrines of England. They were eager to visit shrines such as the Madonna of Ipswich, Our Lady of Woolpit and other smaller sites along the way.

The much-maligned St Walstan survived the verbal abuse of Bishop Bale. His legend outlasted the Reformation and has endured for almost a thousand years, though only in the last few years has the extent of it become apparent in Suffolk. Over the centuries, few if any Suffolk chroniclers included St Walstan in their deliberations, and it was only in 1917 that M. R. James cited an ancient document, which suggested that the saint was born in Blythburgh, rather than at the traditional site in Norfolk. In 1754, when Thomas Gardner published his historical account of Dunwich, Blythburgh and Southwold, mention was made of an early medieval church window to St Walstan at Walberswick, a neighbouring parish of Blythburgh. Lately a number of other Suffolk pre-Reformation icons or references have been identified, including a chapel in St Mary's at Bury St Edmunds and a wood carving high up in the magnificent single hammer beamed roof at Earl Stonham.

Even by the late 1900s there was only one recognised pre-Reformation representation of St Walstan in Suffolk, yet the county now has within its boundaries the only two extant medieval wall paintings depicting the legend. The first is at Cavenham, in the west, and the second at Gisleham, in the east. At Ashby there is a nineteenth-century reference to a series of wall paintings as having been 'all covered with a fresh coat of whitewash' and said to contain 'the History of St Walstan'.

St Walstan was of East Anglian royal blood and, notes an ancient document, 'derived his parentage of distinguished royal stock, his father being called Benedict, his mother Blida'. He was born in 975 and when he was thirteen renounced his wealth and travelled north where he got a job on a farm not far from Norwich. There he worked hard for only his keep; anything more he gave to the poor and needy he met as he went about his work as a farm labourer. His employers, the farmer Nalga and his wife, worried about his taking no wages and pressed him to accept their gift of two white calves.

In his last years Walstan had many visions and finally one that foretold his death. He should instruct Nalga to place his body on a cart, pulled by his two white oxen, which were to be left to go free. Walstan died in 1016 and according to his wishes the oxen were left free to draw the cart unguided. The animals set off and stopped only three times, each time a spring appearing. Finally they came to a stop in the village of Bawburgh where Walstan was buried, and soon afterwards he was declared a saint and patron of farm workers and agriculture.

For several hundred years miracles were said to occur at St Walstan's Well, the water having curative powers so colourfully ridiculed by Bishop Bale. Almost one thousand years later pilgrimage continues to the Church of St Mary and St Walstan. In 1997 the Orthodox Church of St Felix and St Edmund at Felixstowe commissioned a new icon of St Walstan. The following year it was carried in procession on the first Orthodox pilgrimage to Bawburgh.

The scene from the medieval life of St Walstan on the north

wall at Cavenham's Church of St Andrew contains two small figures kneeling at his feet. The identity of these figures, a man and a woman, has caused some discussion: are they characters in the legend of St Walstan? Are they Nalga and his wife, or just passers-by, pilgrims, or perhaps the donors of the painting? One answer could lie in a legend belonging to the nearby village of Woolpit, where there was once a sizeable shrine to Our Lady of Pity. Here, in St Mary's Church is a framed copy of the story of the Green Children of Woolpit as told in the early fifteenth century by William of Newburgh.

One day some farm labourers were at work in a field at Woolpit when they saw a boy and girl who appeared to come out of the pits known as 'Wolfpittes', which existed for the destruction of the wolves that roamed thereabouts. The children, brother and sister, had green bodies and their clothes were made of a strange material. The villagers took them to Sir Richard de Calne, as no one could understand their language. They indicated that they were hungry and the villagers saw they were human and treated them kindly. It transpired that they came from a Christian land where there were churches but there was no sun. That morning, when they were tending their father's sheep they had wandered into a cavern where they heard a noise like the ringing of the bells at Bury St Edmunds Abbey. They tried to search for the source of the music and suddenly found themselves among the reapers in the harvest field at Woolpit, the cavern closing behind them leaving no way back.

Food was offered to the Green Children but they ate nothing until some green beans were brought. The boy was younger than his sister and always appeared tired and lethargic. He never lost his green colour and after a short while he died. His sister, though, grew accustomed to food other than beans and gradually began to lose her green hue. She thrived and was baptised at St Mary's and continued to live in Sir Richard de Calne's household. Eventually, it is said, she married and she never returned to the place where the sun never shone and where there was only a faint twilight to live by. It is to be wondered if the girl had children, and if there might yet be descendants living in Suffolk.

Another Suffolk saint, who was England's patron saint and whose name is forever commemorated in church dedications and the county town of Bury St Edmunds, is Edmund, King and martyr. His image appears in church names (dedications) and on church furniture throughout the county and legends belonging to his ancient cult abound. But it is at Hoxne, a village that sits on the river Dove just south of the Waveney that divides Suffolk from Norfolk, that his story is best known. Like St Walstan, the story of St Edmund is a thousand years old, yet new debate and discovery concerning his cult keeps it alive. Although the church at Hoxne is not dedicated to the ninth-century St Edmund, there were once two Chapels of St Edmund in the parish. Other places in East Anglia lay claim to be the site of his martyrdom but folklore is strongest at Hoxne.

Edmund, son of Alkmund, King of Saxony, was crowned King of East Anglia at Bures in 855 and ruled Suffolk for fourteen years. Then came the Danish invaders and in 870 Edmund led the Saxons to meet the Danes in battle at Thetford. The Danes won and Edmund fled south.

According to legend King Edmund was hiding at Hoxne under a wooden bridge that crossed the stream known today as Goldbrook, a tributary of the river Dove. A newly married couple crossing the bridge saw the glint of Edmund's golden spurs in the water and betrayed him to the Danes. The story goes that Edmund put a curse on any man or woman who crossed the bridge to get married and even over a thousand years later many brides will not cross Goldbrook Bridge on their wedding day.

The betrayed King Edmund was told to renounce Christianity and when he refused his Danish captors bound him to an oak tree on the hill above the stream and shot arrows into his body until he died. His head was chopped off and thrown into the woods, in the hope that his followers would be prevented from giving him a Christian burial. But when the Danes had gone the king's followers recovered the body and searched for his head. One of the searchers heard a cry of 'Here! Here!' and they came to a clearing in the wood where a great wolf guarded the king's head. The animal, having fiercely protected the head, then gave it up for burial. A wooden chapel was built over the spot and so began the cult of St Edmund, King and Martyr. After miracles were recorded at the chapel King Alfred adopted him as his patron saint and East Anglian coins were minted bearing the inscription SC EADMUND REX.

At the beginning of the tenth century the reputation of England's patron saint had grown so strong that his body was removed to 'Boedericsworth' where a magnificent abbey was built. King Canute had a special regard for the saint and in 1032 established a Benedictine monastery foundation there. It became one of the most important and powerful of the English Benedictine abbeys and wrought huge influence on the county's history. 'Boedericsworth' became the borough of St Edmund and is now known as Bury St Edmunds.

Stories and legends grew up around St Edmund at Bury, including the 'Oblation of the White Bull' described by J. M. Matten in *The Cult of St Edmund*:

> There was a curious practice connected with the shrine of St Edmund known as the making of the Oblation of the White Bull. This superstitious rite, believed to have been a relic of East Anglian Paganism, was performed by ladies who desired off-spring. The white bull, decked with ribbons and floral garlands, was brought to the south gate of the Monastery, and led through the streets until the west gate was reached, the interested lady walking by its side, and the monks and townspeople forming an attendant procession.

Once they arrived at the shrine the bull was taken back to its field and the woman went on to pray for the blessing of a child. Any tenant of the 'bull's pasture' held the land on condition that he always kept a white bull in readiness for the ceremony.

At Hoxne a great oak, hallowed as the place of Edmund's martyr-dom, stood for a thousand years until suddenly, on a fine and still morning in October 1848, it fell. A report in the *Bury Post* reported that it was 'entirely demolished', without any apparent cause: '. . . the trunk shivered into several pieces and the immense limbs with the branches lay around in a remarkable manner. The dimensions of the tree were twelve feet in length, six feet in diameter and twenty feet in circumference.' Inside a hollow part of the trunk an arrow-head was found and wood from St Edmund's Oak was used to make a screen, with carvings recording scenes from the life of St Edmund, which was kept for a time in Hoxne Church.

There is hardly a parish in Suffolk that does not have some link to the story of St Edmund, be it church dedication, a screen painting or carving of the wolf guarding his head, or the name of a school, a road or an institution. For several hundred years he was England's patron saint until the cult of St George took on new dimensions for England during the Crusades. The colourful (and dubious) St George began to replace St Edmund as patron saint after the Battle of Agincourt, when, in the words of Shakespeare, Henry V cried, 'God for Harry! England and St George!'

One of the many Suffolk churches which has a reminder of St Edmund is St Peter's at Charsfield, where St Edmund's emblem is found on the panelled base course of the sixteenth-century tower. Charsfield is a small village located a few miles west of Wickham Market astride the Potsford Brook, a tributary of the river Deben, known locally as the 'Black Ditch'. Here farming has been the main-stay of existence since time immemorial, and it was a timeless snap-shot of Suffolk rural life that bought it a place in English literature. In 1969 Ronald Blythe's *Akenfield* was published, an enduring record of life in a Suffolk village in the early twentieth century, which became an overnight best-seller.

Ronald Blythe was born and grew up in Suffolk and at the time that he wrote *Akenfield* lived in Debach, the neighbouring village to Charsfield, not far from Akenham (from which the title derives). The book is the quest for the voice of 'Akenfield' as it sounded during the summer and autumn of 1967. It begins with talk of the farming 'slump' of the 1930s and the memories of men who were children when much of the land changed hands towards the end of the nine-teenth century. The church, as might be expected, was at the centre of life, though in Charsfield there was not just the Church of England but also a Baptist Chapel which shared the village congregation.

This community of just 400 souls illustrated the dual religious lean-ings of conformity and Nonconformity, so much a guiding influence on rural life in East Anglia.

In 'Akenfield' is one 'Mr Thrussel', whose real name was Herman Simper (names were changed in the book, to encourage those who might otherwise remain silent). Herman and Margaret Simper farmed at Brook Farm, a 95-acre holding that was bought from the Duke of Hamilton in 1911 for £20 an acre. It was in the middle of the village and takes its name from the brook that flows past the farmhouse.

Herman was originally in partnership with his brother, Frederick, but the partnership foundered and soon afterwards Herman found himself in sole possession of Brook Farm. What he had not known, however, was that the Duke of Hamilton had already gifted the top of Rookery Meadow to the Church of England to extend the graveyard of Charsfield church. In *Family Fields*, Herman's grandson Robert Simper writes: 'Grandfather Herman had started to attend Charsfield Church, but after this land dispute, he switched his loyalty to the Baptist chapel at the other end of the village. He never forgot or forgave the Duke for the loss of "his" land.'

In *Akenfield*, when 'Mr Thrussel' died his widow went to the Rural Dean to ask that her husband be buried in the churchyard. At first he was surprised, since 'Mr Thrussel' had been 'far from friendly' towards the church during his lifetime. The Baptists had their own burial ground behind the chapel. Why couldn't he be buried there? But this was no church versus chapel debate, as the Rural Dean said:

'He fancied the churchyard,' stated his wife – 'that bit up by the top there.' The penny now dropped. I recalled great battles with Mr Thrussel about a scrap of his land which we had had to take in order to extend the churchyard. He had fought us all along the line but lost. Now he was getting his own back by being buried, as he believed, on his own farm!

In the early seventies the success of *Akenfield* came to the attention of

Peter Hall (later Sir) who was born in Bury St Edmunds, and who recognised in the book the Suffolk of his youth. In collaboration with Ronald Blythe he decided to transcribe *Akenfield* onto film. He would both direct and produce the film, which would be shot in and around Charsfield, Hoo and Woodbridge, using local people as actors. Ronald Blythe himself would play the part of the rector. One of the first villagers he approached was one of Charsfield's best-known residents, Peggy Cole, who agreed to play the part of Mother in the film.

Peggy was born in 1935, the eldest of a large Suffolk family. Her parents were landworkers in Easton, where she was brought up, and in 1953 she married Ernie Cole, a stockman and churchwarden at Charsfield for over thirty years. They began married life at Hoo, and after a short stay at Kesgrave moved to Charsfield. At their council house in Charsfield they created a remarkable cottage garden which opened to the public in 1972 to raise money for charity. (For many years, the 'Akenfield' village sign used in the film stood in the garden.) After Ernie died suddenly in 1980 Peggy and her brother carried on the work in the garden. When it finally closed in 1997 she had raised over £65,000 for various charities.

So it was that in 1974 that the villagers of Charsfield took part in Sir Peter Hall's *Akenfield*, watched with increasing irritation by the widowed Margaret Simper from her vantage point of Brook House, to which she and Herman had retired shortly before his death. The living room window of Brook House afforded a splendid view of the 'T' junction of the village and many hours were spent watching the comings and goings of the village inhabitants as they crossed back and forth in front of Brook House window.

The long drawn out, but nevertheless exciting, goings on of Peter Hall's film crew, with Peggy Cole and the villagers as actors, and unprecedented vehicular activity were almost too much for Margaret. However, she missed not one moment of filming and was exhausted by the number of times she had to forsake her armchair for the upstairs window in order not to miss a thing. She watched critically as the 'funeral procession' went up the hill towards St Peter's, and then back down again; the same procession went down the road towards the Baptist Chapel, and back again. Confusingly the same procedure took place several times and from different approaches. Frustratingly, the church was a few feet out of vision and on at least one occasion she donned hat and coat to watch them climb the hill.

For whatever reason, Margaret Simper did not take part in the film, possibly because of her age, but she was on the edge of her seat when the day came for it to be screened on her much-watched television. However, she was disgusted and commented indignantly throughout on the apparent inaccuracies. The funeral procession did not even go to Charsfield church, it went to Hoo church, and in spite of Peter Hall having visited Charsfield over several months, he still did not appear to know his way around! She also found the switchbacks in time confusing. Writing in *A Country Girl at Heart* Peggy admitted that not everyone in the village liked the film:

> The village had mixed feelings about the film. Some had thought it was going to be just like the book, while others could not understand the switchbacks in time. But on the whole most people enjoyed it. The local press called it 'A classic, down to earth story of a Suffolk village' and gave great praise to Peter Hall and Ronald Blythe.

In 1975 Margaret Simper joined her husband in the churchyard at Charsfield buried, as agreed, in the small piece of land gifted by the Duke of Hamilton to the Church of England in 1911.

In 1984 Peggy Cole received a call from Lady Penn, who said that HRH the Princess Margaret had seen the *Akenfield* film and wanted to visit her garden. During her visit Peggy presented her with a cheque for £100 for the NSPCC, of which the Princess was then President. Besides organising her garden, and writing a weekly column for the *East Anglian Daily Times*, Peggy was awarded an MBE for her charity work in 1992. She was a member of the Parochial Church Council for forty years.

No doubt there were many in *Akenfield* who would have been familiar with the 'wool churches' of Suffolk, churches built of stone but their magnificence deriving from the wealth generated in the golden years of the wool and cloth trade, the finest example being St Peter and St Paul at Lavenham. It was the rich Lavenham clothiers in the late fifteenth century, particularly the Spring family, that paid for the rebuilding and extension of Lavenham church. It has almost cathedral proportions and was rebuilt between 1485 and 1520. Its tower soars to 140 feet and the church itself is almost 200 feet long and 70 feet wide. Inside is an exquisitely carved screen, clerestory windows that have fragments of old glass, a Purbeck marble font and breathtakingly large roof beams, shaped from single oak trees. The sixteenth-century door in the south wall shows linen-fold panelling, with the Spring arms in the spandrels, as yet another reminder of the industry that paid for this grandeur.

Lavenham's heyday came during the 1500s when it was the four-teenth richest town in the country. Wool was dyed in the town and then woven into a thick cloth, for home sale or export. Thomas Spring, who built the south chapel, was one of the richest wool mer-chants in England. A brass in the vestry depicts him, with his wife, four sons and six daughters, in their burial shrouds. Thomas Spring III was head of the family business but he could shear, weave, dye and work as well as any of the workers. He was so successful that when he died, in 1523, his widow was the second richest person in Suffolk, even after paying her taxes!

It is not surprising to find an image of St Blaise at Lavenham, recognisable by the wool comb he is holding. St Blaise was the Bishop of Sebaste in Armenia in the early fourth century and said to have been martyred by being torn by wool combs and then beheaded, and so he became the patron saint of wool combers. St Blaise is found on the parclose screen of Thomas Spring III at the east end of the north aisle of the nave. This is the only figure of St Blaise in Suffolk, although an image on a screen at Eye is thought to be of him, though he holds no wool comb. The feast of St Blaise, 3 February, was always celebrated with annual processions and high spirits not just in Lavenham but at other centres of wool comb-ing such as Bury and Ipswich.

A close second to Lavenham, in terms of wool churches, is St Mary's at Hadleigh. Its spire is the oldest in Suffolk and the frame is seventy feet high, sheathed in lead laid in a herringbone pattern.

It is the fifth largest church in Suffolk, most of its structure dating from the fifteenth century. Just near to the priest's door, on the south wall, was once another entrance through which processions from the town's Guildhall – there were five separate guilds in the town – would enter in medieval times. Hadleigh's association with the wool trade is seen in the arms of the borough, incorporated in 1618, which show wool sacks on the shield and commemorate the town's prosperity which rested on the wool trade from medieval times right up to the seventeenth century.

St Mary's also has a beautiful carving of the wolf guarding the head of St Edmund on a bench end, although the creature has features that suggest the carver had more to say than meets the eye. The wolf's back feet are cloven and it appears to wear a priest's vestments and ornamental collar, with folded wings, suggesting a parody of clerical hypocrisy.

Wool and sheep have always been important to agricultural and industrial Suffolk and in the churchyard of Bradfield Combust – or Burnt Bradfield – lies the tomb of the man responsible for the naming of the Suffolk Sheep. Bradfield Hall was the home of the writer and agriculturist Arthur Young (1741–1820), whose family had lived there since the sixteenth century. In 1797, Young wrote his *General View of Agriculture in the County of Suffolk*, a classic work of its kind. In it he wrote about a sheep then called the Black Face that had evolved from the mating of Norfolk Horn ewes with Southdown rams: 'These ought to be called the Suffolk breed, the mutton has superior texture, flavour, quantity and colour of gravy.'

And so the Black Faces became known as the Suffolk Sheep. The first classes to exhibit the 'Suffolks' were at the 1859 Suffolk Show and the first flock book was published in 1887. It contained forty-six flocks ranging in size from 50 to 1,100 ewes and all forty-six were in East Anglia, thirty-four of them in Suffolk. The oldest flock was that of E. P. and H. Frost of West Wratting, established in 1810. The Suffolk Sheep Society was formed in 1886 at a meeting in Stowmarket and is now the largest sheep breed society in Great Britain.

EIGHTEEN

Boudicca: the warrior queen

THE REPUTATION OF Boudicca, the warrior queen, has long been recognised in Britain, but in Suffolk she is a special heroine. Her story is that of Suffolk's earliest queen and her people, the Iceni tribe, who inhabited those lands that are now called Suffolk. Boudicca has become the byword for a fearless, heroic woman, and tales of her determined fight against Roman domination still inspire writers of both novels and non-fiction. The Iceni tribe, those early inhabitants of Suffolk and Norfolk, was indeed led by a warrior queen whose name meant 'victory' and who was Suffolk's first champion.

Boudicca, known to the Victorians as Boadicea, was born into a royal family around 26 AD and married the Icenian king, Prasutagus. After the Roman invasion of AD 43, the Iceni lived under a rule that grew ever more harsh and oppressive, encroaching on their way of life and their freedom. Although real power lay with the Romans, Prasutagus had initially welcomed the invaders as allies in the constant struggle with his western neighbours, the troublesome Catuvellauni. In return for his collusion he was allowed to keep his title and position. The Iceni were a proud and independent people and even under Roman rule minted their own coins. But in AD 47 came the first rift with Rome. The governor of the province wanted to tighten control on the Britons and the Iceni began to feel the heavy hand of repression on their nominal, but all-important, independence. The Roman occupiers had betrayed the special relationship that Prasutagus thought he had secured for his people.

Huge Roman forts were built on Iceni land and young Iceni men were forced to leave their homesteads when conscripted into the Roman army against their will. Taxes were levied in the form of grain, which in poor harvests meant the prospect of starvation among the native tribes. Hatred of the invaders began to rise dangerously and talk of revolution was in the air.

In AD 60 King Prasutagus died and with him went the fragile protection that the Iceni still enjoyed. In his will Prasutagus left the kingdom to Boudicca but tried to safeguard at least some of his estates by including the Emperor Nero as joint heir with his daughters. As a mark of her new authority the widowed queen caused the Devil's Dyke to be built on the western boundary of Iceni lands. It was intended to be a barrier against a landward invasion by the powerful and hostile Catuvellauni tribes. She also founded a Royal Stud near Exning, better known today as Newmarket Racecourse. All in vain: the Romans dismissed any rights of an occupied people to have a legitimate say in their affairs. The procurator, Catus Decianus, sent his men to Suffolk where they pillaged the countryside. All Icenian possessions were sequestered and Decianus and others called in monies formerly distributed by the late Emperor Claudius to ensure local co-operation with the invasion. They were not gifts, he argued, but loans and subsidies to be repaid. Hoards of silver coins and treasure were hastily buried but never retrieved by their owners. Several hundred years were to pass before the riches and treasures of the Iceni were seen again.

Next, the Icenian estates were confiscated and the owners

made slaves. When Boudicca protested she was publicly flogged. Her two teenage daughters, far from gaining their inheritance, were raped by Roman soldiers as a lesson to the tribe that they were no longer in charge of their own destiny, and Boudicca was forced to watch the humiliating spectacle.

Boudicca was enraged and resolved that the Iceni would not be conquered. She was transformed into a fierce enemy of Rome and, after witnessing the outrage against her daughters and the Roman contempt for her status as queen, became a resolute and fiery defender of women's rights. She inspired not only men to join her cause, but also many women who swelled the ranks of the forces that followed her into battle against Roman domination.

Intelligence came to her that the bulk of the Roman army was in north Wales. The military governor of the province, Suetonius Paullinus, needed to extinguish sustained antagonism from the natives of Anglesey, which was constantly whipped up by the Druid priesthood. Now was the time to strike. Loathing towards Rome had reached such a pitch that Boudicca had no trouble in marshalling the semblance of an army. She effortlessly established herself as leader of an Icenian uprising, forming an alliance with the neighbouring Trinovantes (in what is now south Suffolk) to swell her ranks. She gathered her followers and headed south towards Camulodunum (Colchester), the capital city of the new Roman province of Britannia, collecting new recruits as she went. Where necessary she liberated the men and women of her tribe from their Roman masters by burning and destroying homes and settlements, slaughtering some seventy thousand people as she went and leaving a trail of destruction in her wake. Any Briton believed to have collaborated with the Romans was singled out for special cruelty. She took no prisoners but slaughtered those who fell into rebel hands by crucifixion, hanging, burning or the sword.

Boudicca became a feared and powerful leader as she rallied her troops along the way. She was described by one Roman historian as 'a terrifying-looking woman with fierce eyes and a harsh voice'. The Roman historian Dio Cassius described her thus:

A Briton of Royal race and breathing more than female spirit. She was of great size and most terrible of aspect, most savage of countenance and harsh of voice, having a profusion of yellow hair which fell down to her hips, and wearing a large golden collar; she wore a many-coloured floating vest drawn close about her bosom and over this a thick mantle fastened by a clasp.

She also carried a spear that she could wield as well as any man, often with greater strength and accuracy. A huge bronze statue of Boudicca and her daughters stands near the Houses of Parliament in London. It shows how her image has come down to us through the eyes of the Victorians, who saw mirrored in her the prophetic model for their own queen's spread of empire, and made her their heroine. The rearing, un-reined horses draw Boudicca's war chariot as she heads south, through what is now Suffolk, to defy her Roman conquerors and regain freedom for the native Britons. The spectacular use of war chariots, and the standards of horsemanship displayed by the Iceni had impressed even Julius Caesar when he first came to Britain in 55 BC. A metal hoard found at Westhall evidences intricate harness mounts from a horsedrawn chariot of Boudicca's time.

At Camulodunum the tribesmen found the Roman garrison poorly armed. The absent governor Suetonius Paullinus had left the garrison manned by only a handful of troops. After a two-day siege the Romans were easily driven back through the town to take refuge in the Temple of Claudius. Having successfully manoeuvred the enemy neatly into a single place, Boudicca's troops, by then numbering about 230,000, attacked. Dio Cassius says that before the battle Boudicca and her daughters drove around the troops in their chariot, exhorting them to fight: 'We British are used to women commanders in war. I am descended from mighty men . . . consider how many of you are fighting, and why! Then will you win this battle or perish. This is what I, a woman, intend to do. Let the men live in slavery if they will!'

The Temple of Claudius dominated the forum and was so grandiose that even the Romans mocked it. The Iceni saw it as a symbol of Roman tyranny and resented the enormous sums of money squandered by men chosen as 'priests' who were no more than thugs and bullies. The temple was a tempting prize – to destroy it was significant for their cause, and the prospect, Boudicca knew, would sustain their anger and their frenzy in battle.

After a bloody battle the Boudiccan rebels triumphed, destroying the temple and razing it to the ground. The victorious Boudicca ordered the burning of what was left of the town and her followers grabbed as much loot as they could carry. Camulodunum was theirs!

The rebel queen addressed her troops. They had won the battle but not the war. They would, she promised, go on to destroy first the burgeoning supply and trade centre of Londinium (London) and then Verulamium (St Albans), whose inhabitants had consorted with the Romans in return for a status almost equal to that of a full Roman citizen. They would kill the enemy and its collaborators and regain lands, property and rights for the native people. But the rebel forces were in truth no more than an undisciplined and untrained bunch of men and women more used to the peaceful ways of rural existence than fighting. They had courage and cause, but they were no match for the professional Roman army. After successfully attacking Londinium Boudicca's rabble set off to do the same at Verulamium, but there they were to feel the superior power of their oppressors and the weight of their own fatigue.

On hearing the news that Camulodunum had fallen, Suetonius Paullinus brought his campaign in Wales to an abrupt halt. At a spot still unidentified, he and Boudicca met in battle in the spring of AD 61. On one side stood the whole of Legion XX, part of Legion XIV and an assortment of auxiliaries under Roman command. On the other side was a ragtag army of Boudicca's native Britons, exhausted and with no war strategy beyond rebellion. Their only protection was a line of carts and wagons, containing their followers, and they had no body armour to protect them from Roman swords. Like many ancient warriors they painted their bodies with woad, which had antiseptic properties and for naked fighters helped to protect wounds from infection.

At the final battle Boudicca saw her followers scattered and thousands killed by the now regrouped Romans. It is said that Boudicca and her daughters took poison rather than suffer further indignities at Roman hands, but in any case her troops turned away from Verulamium. They retreated back into Suffolk, a spent and demoralised force, their queen vanquished and the Roman oppressors triumphant and vengeful. In small groups they crawled back to their farmsteads and villages.

No one has ever found out where Boudicca's body is buried. Like King Arthur, she has many legendary burial sites but no evidence has ever been put forward to authenticate any of them. Her lasting memorial is the jolt that her rebellion gave to Roman imperialism. The Emperor Nero decreed that new conquests be put on hold for almost ten years and it was reputed that he even contemplated withdrawing from Britain in the face of such ferocious opposition.

For many years to come the Iceni had to watch while Rome consolidated its hold on their lands. They saw Gariannonum (Burgh Castle) built and extended to form one of a chain of fortresses stretching along the coast. The remains of its massive walls are still visible today. At Pakenham a fort was built that was defended by triple ditches and commanded the ford where the Peddars Way crossed the river Blackbourn. Walton Castle, near Felixstowe, became a major Roman fortification, and a network of roads was built across Suffolk linking important settlements to the ports. Pye Street connected Ipswich with the old northern Iceni territories, now Norfolk, and for westward access the ancient route of Peddars Way was improved and straightened, while the Icknield Way traversed Suffolk from Newmarket to Thetford. The Roman town of Icklingham was built sprawling across the countryside, and innumerable villas constructed on farms and in villages. Towns grew up at Coddenham, Long Melford, Knodishall and Wenhaston, interspersed with military sites and smaller satellite villages that sprang up to service the ongoing Romanisation of Britain. Camulodunum was resurrected.

Boudicca's last stand against Suetonius Paullinus became a landmark of the Roman occupation of Britain and sealed the country's fate for the next 350 years. Gradually the boundaries between Roman and Iron Age Britain were blurred and the native people, including the Iceni and Trinovantes, became Romano-British. Evidence of Roman occupation turns up in almost every village in Suffolk and ancient settlements are still being revealed today, long-forgotten Roman villas picked out from aerial surveys.

Boudicca's Dyke remains highly visible and runs between the two racecourses at Newmarket, the 'July' and the 'Rowley Mile'. This eight-mile long earth mound is well known to the thousands of race-goers who visit each year and it is also a very popular hike for walkers. Generations have stood, and will stand, on the Devil's Dyke very early in the morning to watch the sun rise across the heath, silhouetting the stable lads as they begin exercising the horses and adding another new day to the long traditions begun in AD 61.

Every so often a hoard of treasure is unearthed, as at West Row near Mildenhall, where a ploughman turned up Roman silver. A Money Tree stood at Benacre, so called because 900 Roman coins were found buried at its roots. At Eye a hoard of 600 coins, buried to save them from seizure by the Romans, was discovered in the 1780s. Some of these hoards were hidden during the Boudicca period and were buried in pots sealed with cloths of flax or hemp. They contain the silver coins of the Iceni mint, and at Lakenheath a solitary gold issue of Icenian King Antedios (c. AD 25–50) has been found, together with 410 Icenian coins and 65 Roman denarii.

Even by AD 407, when the Romans began to relinquish direct control of Britain, the people of Suffolk were still protecting their property from confiscation, though by then they were almost Roman themselves. At Hoxne a vast number of coins and objects, all of gold and silver, were buried at about that time. This treasure, the greatest Roman hoard ever to have been found in Britain, lay undiscovered until 1992 when it was unearthed by chance. Eric Lawes was using his metal detector to look for a friend's hammer and found more than he bargained for. Realising this was more than just a few odd coins, Mr Lawes reported the find to the Suffolk Archaeological Unit and the following day a team arrived to mount an emergency excavation of the site. By nightfall all the objects had been recovered and taken to the British Museum. The discovery caused a sensation and later, on 3 September 1993, it was declared treasure-trove at a coroner's inquest in Lowestoft, thereby earning Mr Lawes a £1.75 million payout.

There were twenty-nine pieces of gold jewellery, including necklaces, finger-rings and bracelets, and a body chain joined front and back with decorative plaques of pearl and amethyst. There were silver items, including a prancing tigress and pepper pots and beautifully crafted ladles and spoons, and 14,870 coins. The Hoxne Hoard gives a glimpse of the immense wealth of a Suffolk estate owner and his family in late Roman times but no clue as to why it was hidden. It was packed with care, the delicate silver bowls separated by padding, and placed in the ground in wooden boxes rather than being hastily buried. Who knows what else is lying beneath the earth, waiting to be discovered?

The Romans finally retreated in about AD 450 but by then there was nothing left of the Iceni or Trinovantes and Queen Boudicca had passed into legend. A few years later new adventurers – the Saxons – invaded Suffolk shores to make their mark on the landscape and a fresh mix of blood would run in native veins. Not long after that the southern 'folk' became the 'south folk' and so the name Suffolk was formed and the county divided from Norfolk by the rivers Waveney and Little Ouse, while the Stour formed the barrier with Essex, the East Saxons.

In 1907 a lad by the name of Arthur Godbold went fishing in the village of Rendham, which lies on the river Alde. He caught nothing all afternoon, but then saw what he thought was something round, almost the size of a football, at the river's edge. Arthur and his friends at Rendham School knew that something had previously been seen in that part of the river that ran through the farm meadows where his father was the bailiff. He ran and told his father that he had seen what looked like the much-discussed object. It was lying sideways by the bank and with the help of a hoe the boy and his father fished it out. 'We could see straight-away that it wasn't a human head', said Arthur many years later, 'but I took it home and whitewashed it, and stood it on the wall outside the house. It remained there for some time and no one seemed to show any special interest in it.'

Gradually the head was all but forgotten. At the time it had been the talk of the village, and at first it was a novelty but after a few years everyone got used to it sitting on the wall and the whitewash began to wear off. Arthur and his schoolboy friends tired of the story of how they had found a head in the river, until one day a man turned up from nearby Benhall Lodge and asked if he could buy it. Arthur was thrilled to receive five shillings for the head and that was the last he heard of it for many years.

The man from Benhall Lodge, however, had been well schooled in the legend of Boudicca and the rebellious Iceni. John Chambers, headmaster at Benhall village school, used to tell his pupils thrilling stories of Queen Boudicca and her daughters and their courageous stand against the Roman invaders. One of the stories concerned the Battle of Pipnen Hill, in Rendham, when Boudicca was reputed to have sailed up the river Alde in search of new recruits for her army. The river was much wider then than now and Mr Chambers told how the men and women of Rendham and Benhall had fought the local Romans and joined the queen in her advance on Camulodunum. Was it possible that this bronze, head-shaped object could have something to do with the Icenian uprising of AD 60?

The head was cleaned and taken to Ipswich Museum where it caused no small excitement. It was just conceivable that this was a bronze head of Claudius not unlike that which had been looted from the Temple of Claudius at Camulodunum by Boudicca's troops in AD 60. It was sent to London where the British Museum confirmed that it was, in fact, a head of Claudius and that it had once been part of a life-sized statue of the emperor, mounted on a horse, which had stood in the temple at Camulodunum.

How had the head of Claudius come to be in the river at Rendham? Did the fleeing Iceni throw it there, or was it dropped by accident? The head was taken as a trophy but once the rebels were routed it would have become something of a liability. To be found by the Romans in possession of such a thing would have meant certain death to whoever possessed it. In the wake of their defeat by Governor Paullinus many Icenian and Trinovantian settlements had been laid waste by the full force of the Roman army.

Such incriminating evidence would surely have meant the destruction of the whole village.

Had a Rendham family, whose son or father had taken part in the assault on the temple, purposely hidden the head? Perhaps they hoped that one day the Romans would be defeated and the head of Claudius could be retrieved and claimed as a trophy of victory? Or was it simply lost by accident, or even thrown into the river in desperation at the situation the conquered people then found themselves in?

In pre-Roman Britain there had been a cult of the severed head, while Iron Age Britain had customs of throwing objects into water, especially rivers. It was many years after the Roman invasion before these ancient rites and rituals were abandoned or adapted. A large bronze head of the Emperor Hadrian, similar to that of Claudius, was recovered from the river Thames near London Bridge. The destruction of idols was seen as a duty by the very early Christians, who disfigured them before throwing them into the water. Perhaps the head of Claudius was taken from another hiding place and a ceremony performed, in Rendham on the banks of the river Alde, to dispose of it.

We shall never know how or why it got into the river Alde but certainly the head of the Emperor Claudius was not retrieved by whoever brought it there from Camulodunum. Instead it was found almost two thousand years later by a Rendham schoolboy, taken in due course to Ipswich Museum and so into the annals of history. In 1965 the head was sent to Sotheby's by the trustees of Miss Holland, on whose land it had been found, where it was sold for £15,500, the highest price fetched by an antiquity since the end of the Second World War. It was bought by Mr John Hewett, a London dealer, acting on behalf of the British Museum, where it has been ever since, with replicas at Ipswich, Colchester and Rendham.

A reporter from the *Leiston Observer* tracked down Arthur Godbold, then aged seventy-two, who lived with his wife in the village of Gillingham, just outside Beccles. 'You've come about the head,' he said. 'I had forgotten about it until the other day when my former employer came to me and said, "Arthur, your head is in the paper."' He said he had no regrets about selling the emperor's head for five shillings. Calling in his wife, whom he had met when she worked as a maid at Rendham Vicarage, Arthur settled down to retell the story of Boudicca, Queen of the Iceni, and how as a schoolboy he had found the bronze head of the Emperor Claudius in the river Alde.

BIBLIOGRAPHY

JOURNALS AND PERIODICALS:

Bury Free Press
East Anglian Daily Times
Evening Star
Lowestoft Journal

BOOKS:

Blythe, Ronald, *Akenfield*, 1969
Bruni, Georgina, *You Can't Tell The People*, 2000
Butcher, David, *Following the Fishing*, 1987
Butler, Brenda, Street, Dot and Randles, Jenny, *Sky Crash*, 1986
Cobbold, Richard, *History of Margaret Catchpole*, 1845
Dymond, David and Northeast, Peter, *A History of Suffolk*, 1995
Fincham, Paul, *The Suffolk We Live In*, 1976
Football Monthly's World Cup Souvenir, 1966
Freeman, Roger A., *The Friendly Invasion*, 1992
Mee, Arthur, *Suffolk*, 1949
Ramsey, Alfred, *Talking Football*, 1952
Redstone, Lilian J., *Ipswich Through The Ages*, 1969
Scarfe, Norman, *The Suffolk Guide*, 1988
Sealey, Paul R., *The Boudican Revolt Against Rome*, 1997
Simper, Robert, *Family Fields*, 1999
Smith, Graham, *Suffolk Airfields in the Second World War*, 1995

Thompson, Leonard P., *Smugglers of the Suffolk Coast*, 1968

Twinch, Carol, *Tithe War 1918–1939*, 2001

Wallace, Doreen, *The Tithe War*, 1934

Warren, Larry and Robbins, Peter, *Left at East Gate*, 1997